BEGINNING YOUR ENNEAGRAM JOURNEY

Lindsay —
Good luck, have fun,
be brave.

Your Pal —
Leah

BEGINNING YOUR ENNEAGRAM JOURNEY

With Self-observation

Loretta Brady, M.A., M.S.W.

Send all inquiries to:
Tabor Publishing
200 East Bethany Drive
Allen, Texas 73002–3804

Printed in the United States of America

ISBN 0-88347-284-8

1 2 3   4 5 6   98 97 96 95 94

Contents

Introduction

W ho am I? Who are you? Why are we here on this earth together? These are questions which we ask ourselves and each other all the time. Although we never get complete answers, we keep asking. Who is this person I call "Me?" What makes me the kind of person I am? Why am I such a mystery to myself? What am I doing here in this world? What is the purpose of my life? And who are you? Some parts of your person make sense to me. Other parts are totally puzzling. Why do you feel, think, and do things differently than I do? I want to understand you so that I can relate honestly to you. I want to survive and grow with you in this world. And so our questioning goes on and on, each of us hoping someday to discover the answers.

The fields of philosophy, spirituality and psychology have all been very influential in providing some answers for me. First of all, I love the "why" questions of philosophy. I always have and I suspect I always will. There is a mixture in me of intense curiosity and mental playfulness. These energies continually move me forward in a never-ending and delightful search for meaning. Secondly, my spiritual sense of God is for me the center of all creation. I especially enjoy those phrases for God which attempt to describe the indescribable reality of God: I am who am, the uncaused cause, the prime mover, and so forth. This is who God is to me, the beginning and the end of all life. God is the cause and purpose for our being. This sense of God is the bedrock of meaning for me. Finally, psychology has also helped me with its explanations of the human developmental process, our genetic influences, and the stages of growth throughout life. It has helped me to understand something of our human nature and the life process.

For most of my adult life, I had combined psychological and spiritual influences for my personal journey as well as for my professional work. Then I was introduced to the Enneagram theory which offered me a framework that can encompass both the spiritual and the psychological. The Enneagram is not, of course, *the* truth. Nor is it a greater truth than those discovered by psychology and those revealed to us spiritually. Rather, the Enneagram theory provides an overall framework which can bring these two disciplines or areas together. This deepens our understanding of both psychology and spirituality. The Enneagram has provided me with many answers to the questions: Who am I? And who are you? It is because I have gained so much from the Enneagram that I would like to pass on to you my own understanding of it.

Now we are faced with a new set of questions. What is the Enneagram? How is this word pronounced? What does it mean? Everyone seems to ask about its meaning and pronunciation first: Any-a-what? "Any-a-gram" is the way this unusual looking word is pronounced. It is a combination of two Greek words. *Ennea* means "nine." And *gram* means a "unit of measure," or a "measuring point." The two Greek derivatives together mean "nine points" or "nine positions."

When the Enneagram theory is applied to human nature, it suggests that there are nine different vantage points from which we humans view reality. There are nine ways of looking at reality. From our particular views of reality will flow our motivations, our thoughts, our feelings, and our choices of action. To illustrate this concept, take the example of two individuals who differ in their views of reality. One person feels that what is most important in life is connecting with other *people*. Another might give the greatest value to connecting *ideas* rather than people. I'm sure you can imagine how these two individuals will differ in their motivations, thoughts, feelings and actions. It will be evident in the way that each one lives life. Throughout this book, you will encounter these differences as you come to know the nine fundamental views of reality.

The precise origin of the Enneagram theory is unknown today. As we study it together, we will probably get some sense of how it can be seen as a summary of universal truths. For example, we all know that 2 + 2 = 4. This is a universal truth. No one invented this truth. It was always so. It is a fact that was simply uncovered one day many centuries ago. The same thing is true of the Enneagram. It was probably not invented by any one person. It was simply uncovered. In our 20th Century there are two people who claim to have uncovered what they have described as an ancient oral tradition. George Ivanovitch Gurdjieff, a Russian thinker, organized a school in the 1920s in Paris, "The Institute for the Harmonious Development of Man." There he taught the basic principles of the Enneagram theory. Gurdjieff, himself, claims to have learned these from others in the course of his travels. However, he is considered one of those most responsible for uncovering and developing the ideas basic to the Enneagram theory. Some years later, Oscar Ichazo also began teaching the Enneagram in Bolivia and Chile. He more fully developed the descriptions of each of the nine positions and greatly expanded the understanding of the Enneagram. While he was still teaching in South America, however, many North Americans traveled to his school to learn from him. They brought the Enneagram theory back to the United States for use in their studies and work. Eventually, Ichazo founded the Arica Institute in New York City. Slowly, the Enneagram has spread.

The publication of written presentations of the Enneagram did not occur until the 1970s. Once the Enneagram moved from an oral tradition into a written form of transmission, its popularity spread even more rapidly. Today, many people are presenting the Enneagram in workshops and publications. Each presenter seems to bring something unique to the basic theory. While this divergence of presentations may seem to be confusing, I see it as a richer and fuller approach to reaching many different people.

The diversity of presentations mirrors the theory itself. The theory maintains that we are all different and at the same time we are also the same. In a similar way, the Enneagram belongs to no one person or group. It has come down to us today through many centuries and many different traditions. It is a set of truths about human nature, which are simply true. But these truths are capable of different presentations and an ever deeper understanding.

As we become more familiar with the Enneagram, we gradually realize that it simply describes what is already a reality. We are often not listening, not looking, or simply not awake to the life that is in us and around us. Involvement with the Enneagram will wake us up to the realities of who we are, how each of us views life, and consequently, how each of us lives life. It will also give us a glimpse into the views of reality different from our own. This will help us to understand others.

There are two ways to approach the Enneagram. One way is to study it as a theory. The other way is to use it to help find the answers to: Who am I? Who are you? In this book, I hope to combine both approaches. In each of the following chapters, I will discuss a part of the Enneagram theory. Then I will offer you, the reader, some examples and questions to ponder and respond to in your own way.

Finally, in referring to the nine different basic views of reality, I will be using the Enneagram position numbers one through nine. Some presenters have chosen to give each of these views a title or name. Sometimes this can be descriptively helpful. However, I have found that it also can mislead people into over-simplifications and misunderstandings of the Enneagram. So instead I will refer to the *Number One person*, the *Number Two person*, and so forth. As we begin, let me wish you a growthful journey. *Bon Voyage!*

CHAPTER ONE

To Know Ourselves and To Understand Others

KNOWING OURSELVES AT A DEEPER LEVEL

The idea of knowing oneself is as old as the ancient, Greek axiom: "Know Thyself." It is also as current as any local magazine stand. In many magazines, we very often find quizzes, such as "Ten Questions to Know Yourself." Or "Twenty Questions to Improve Your Relationships." So many of us buy these magazines, and we have great fun taking these quizzes. It has always seemed a bit strange to me that, although we are so fascinated with knowing ourselves, we often settle for knowing just a few traits.

Actually, quizzes can measure only our traits and preferences. For example, you like to go to the movies, he prefers to go to the opera, and I would rather stay at home and read a book. This factual information doesn't really tell us much until we ask: *Why* are these our choices? When we ask "why" we are looking for what is beneath our choices. At that deeper level we find our motivations. It is at this level of self-awareness that we begin to weave together the fabric of our personal identity. All the bits and pieces of who we are and always have been come together and help us recognize our personal basic view of reality. This explains to us why we each "do life" in the way we do.

UNDERSTANDING OTHERS AS "OTHER"

The fact is that we each have a different way in which we "do life." This variety comes from our different views of reality. In order to know ourselves and to understand others, we must uncover our views of reality. How can the Enneagram help us in this process? First of all, unlike the quizzes and questionnaires, the Enneagram can help us go deeper and ask the "why" questions which help us to uncover our own motivational level. The Enneagram process gradually brings all of our various parts into a composite whole. This will go a long way towards answering that question: Who am I?

The Enneagram, as we have said, can also help us understand others. We cannot know others as we can know ourselves. They are simply "other." But we can go a long way towards understanding others. When I put all the pieces of me together, I make psychological sense. I might not make logical sense to someone else, but to me these pieces make up a whole system that fits together. And, although your basic view of reality may be different from mine, you too make psychological sense. It's a different sense from mine, but it is a certain kind of total sense that is vital to who you are. And if I can understand only that much about you, then we can relate to each other.

I can also have empathy for you when things are not going well in your life. Maybe you're out of sorts. Well, with the help of the Enneagram, perhaps now I will not become so confused. Or I will not simply react with anger to your moodiness. Instead I will be able to understand something of *why* you are the way you are. Then I can freely choose my response to you. So the Enneagram has two very important gifts for each of us. It can offer us a sense of knowing and accepting ourselves. At the same time it can help us to understand and empathize with others.

DIFFERENT VIEWS OF THE SAME REALITY

To start getting a sense of what is meant by the different points of viewing reality, I would like to suggest an example to you. Let's say that there is a group of ten people who are going to an event together. They are walking toward the entrance of the place where the event is to be held. Suddenly one of them trips on a cracked sidewalk and falls. Each of the others will react differently to this experience.

The Number One person:	"It's inexcusable to leave a sidewalk in such poor condition."
The Number Two person:	"Awwwh. You poor thing. Let me help you up."
The Number Three person:	"Here, I'm good at this sort of thing. I'll do it."
The Number Four person:	"I fell like this once, and I was in bed for two weeks afterwards."
The Number Five person:	"Isn't it interesting how everyone is reacting differently to the same event?"
The Number Six person:	"Are you okay? Oh gosh, now we are all going to be late. This is awful. What should we do?"
The Number Seven person:	"Wow! What a fall! Hey, but you'll be up and dancing in no time."
The Number Eight person:	"I'm going to get hold of the building manager and demand that this be rectified immediately."
The Number Nine person:	"Calm down, Everyone. Everything's going to be all right. Let's not get too excited."

As you can gather from this "cracked sidewalk" story, the same event can provoke different responses from each person. This is because each one is viewing the reality of this occurrence in a different way. Differing views of reality produce different responses to reality. Right now you may actually be identifying with one of the responses given in the example. And you may also be wondering how the responses of the others could seem so out of touch with what is happening.

I think we are all a bit reluctant to admit that "my view of reality" is not the only valid view of reality. So we often say things like: "If you would just see it *my* way . . . do it *my* way!" Or: "*Anyone* would feel the way I do. . . . Anyone would do what I did." We have this way of moving out from our own attitudes, feelings and actions to envelope all of humanity. It's another way of saying: "The way I feel about it . . . judge it . . . view it . . . is the way it is."

I don't think that I have ever met a person who in some way doesn't tend to do this. It's a temptation from which we all suffer. We tend to think that because we experience the world a certain way, that's the way it must be. This temptation is simply a part of the human condition. It comes from that time in our lives when we once thought we ruled the world and were the center of all life: our royal infancy years.

MANY VIEWS AND THE WHOLE PICTURE

In my experience with the Enneagram, one of the things that has become apparent to me is this. My view is only a part of the total view of reality. Every other person's view is also a part of that same reality. So I need to open to others who share with me in the human condition. I must ask each of them: "What is your view?" Then, when all of these views are put together, I will no longer struggle for supremacy over the others. Rather, I will join them in complementarity. Your view adds to my view, and vice versa. All views together give me the whole view of reality, the full feeling of life, the total experience of humanness.

This is what I think the Enneagram has been doing for me and what it can do for you. It can help us know ourselves at a deeper level. It can reveal to each of us our basic view of reality. When we come to know ourselves at this deeper level, we will be able to move forward on our life journey of growth. We will be better able to accept ourselves as we are.

This will free our energies from the constant work of pretending to be someone we're not. Then we will be able to make new choices to flourish and grow. And beyond that, the Enneagram can help us understand that one person's basic view of reality is different from that of others. Other people have different ways of living life. They have differing ideas of who they are, why they do what they do. If I can only recognize this, and learn to appreciate others as well as appreciate myself, I will definitely be enriched as a person. I will not be simply taking part in my one segment of the human experience, but I will participate in the fullness of humanity.

Consider the following poem:

THE BLIND MEN AND THE ELEPHANT
by John Godfrey Saxe
A HINDOO FABLE

It was six men of Indostan
To learning much inclined,
Who went to see the Elephant
(Though all of them were blind),
That each by observation
Might satisfy his mind.

The First approached the Elephant
And happening to fall
Against his broad and sturdy side,
At once began to bawl:
"God bless me! but the Elephant
Is very like a wall!"

The Second, feeling of the tusk,
Cried, "Ho! what have we here
So very round and smooth and sharp?
To me 'tis mighty clear
This wonder of an Elephant

Is very like a spear!"
The Third approached the animal,
And happening to take
The squirming trunk within his hands,
Thus boldly up and spake:
"I see," quoth he, "the Elephant
Is very like a snake!"

The Fourth reached out an eager hand,
And felt about the knee
"What most this wondrous beast is like
Is mighty plain," quoth he;
" 'Tis clear enough the Elephant
Is very like a tree!"

The Fifth who chanced to touch the ear,
Said: "Even the blindest man
Can tell what this resembles most;
Deny the fact who can,
This marvel of an Elephant
Is very like a fan!"

The Sixth no sooner had begun
About the beast to grope,
Then, seizing on the swinging tail
That fell within his scope,
"I see," quoth he, "the Elephant
Is very like a rope!"

And so these men of Indostan
Disputed loud and long,
each in his own opinion
Exceeding stiff and strong,
Though each was partly in the right,
And all were in the wrong!

Arna Bontemps, *Hold Fast To Dreams: Poems Old
& New* (Chicago: Follett, 1989.) Used by permission.

CHAPTER TWO

From the Beginning . . .
We Are Who We Are

DIFFERENT MOTIVATIONS

As we continue the journey inward, you may begin to wonder about *how* and *when* and *why* we each chose our different views of reality. The totally true answer to those questions is that no one is really sure. However, thanks to psychological research and spiritual teachings we do have some possible answers.

I would like to describe what I think might very well be the how-when-why of our different choices and growth processes. This description comes from my understanding of developmental psychology and my belief in certain spiritual teachings. I would like to stress that these are only *my* understandings and *my* beliefs. I am very aware that my own highly personal view of reality has led me to be selective in choosing only certain portions of what has been said. I do not see the human life and growth process in exactly the same way as others who might describe it. We each have our own view of reality. So please feel free to be selective in choosing from what I say before integrating it into your own individual approach.

I believe that you and I first came into existence when we were created by God. It's impossible to know if it was when we were conceived in a physical way through our parents' sexual union. Or was it possibly even earlier than that in a moment when God first conceived of us as creatures? In any case, we each had a beginning. This was at least from the moment of physical conception, and perhaps even before this in a way we can not understand.

I also believe that from the beginning of our existence much of who we are as individuals was already determined. Today, we know that long before we are born our DNA is already imprinted with many physical determinants such as hair and eye color, as well as a predisposition to certain diseases. In a similar manner, I think, our preferential way of relating to the world was already determined. This does not mean we have no freedom of will. We still remain free to make all the choices that life will offer. However, I will make my choices from a certain vantage point. Other people will freely choose from their other vantage points. We may even make the same choice as others, but it will be from different motivations.

AN EXAMPLE:

Suppose there is a person lying at the side of a road and bleeding. Imagine that nine different people come by and all of them choose to help.

The Number One person chooses to help by fixing a tourniquet while reprimanding the imagined perpetrator.

The Number Two person chooses to help by gently wiping away the blood and dirt while holding the person in a comforting position.

The Number Three person chooses to help by organizing some of the onlookers to build a stretcher.

The Number Four person chooses to help by sympathizing with the wounded person in pain.

The Number Five person chooses to help by examining the wounded person to see just what is wrong, speculating on what might have happened.

The Number Six person chooses to help by going to call for the police and an ambulance.

The Number Seven person chooses to help by distracting the panic-stricken onlookers with conversation and stories.

The Number Eight person chooses to help by holding the crowd back from the accident scene.

The Number Nine person chooses to help by calming the frightened and angry onlookers with soothing remarks.

All nine people chose to help. Yet each offered a different kind of help. They each offered from their own individual resources. Perhaps on other occasions when there would have been more time to consider a choice of action, they each might have chosen several ways to help. However, this was a sudden occurrence, a crisis. On these occasions we act instinctively, precisely from our own natural and innate giftedness.

I think that each of us comes into existence with a particular giftedness. I believe this giftedness is meant to reflect one facet of God who created us. The Bible says that we are made "in the image and likeness of God." I take this to mean that through our personhood we are to bring into the world a finite image, likeness or reflection of an infinite God. And this is our gift.

INTERPRETING THE INFLUENCES OF CHILDHOOD

Moving on to another approach, let's consider what effect the events of our childhood had on the development of who each of us is today. Psychology claims that it is our childhood years and the events which take place in those years that define who we are as persons. While I do agree that the whole process of childhood affects the later stages of our lives, I don't think that particular events define us. Rather, I think *we define or interpret the events according to our already determined view of reality*. For example, if you were to ask several grown children from the same family what was the most stressful event in their family's history, they might well all report different occurrences: "When the twins were born. . . . When all five of us were in grade school together. . . . When we moved. . . . When Mom went back to college. . . . When my oldest brother went into the army. . . . There really wasn't much stress at all. . . . It was all stressful."

Another example of the same idea comes from my own childhood. In this case one major event happened which *did* affect all of us more than anything else. Yet the significance we each gave to it varies from one person in my family to another. When I was very young the event which affected everyone in my family the most was the death of my father. There were several other young brothers and sisters besides myself in the family. All of us would agree, I'm sure, that the death of our father was the most important event of our childhood. However, we each defined it differently. Consequently, each of us feels we were affected differently by it. I think you will see what I mean in comparing the following reactions:

"I loved him but I was relieved when he died. He always expected so much from me."

"I still remember the day Dad died as the saddest day of my life. It still hurts."

"It's still so sad to me that it ever happened, but I did learn very early in life how to make the best of bad situations."

"I was so scared because no one told me it was going to happen. As a child I thought that if I had known it was going to happen then I would have been ready for it."

"It felt as if I got the wind knocked out of me, but it sure challenged me to grow up."

"I felt cheated out of a father, and I still feel cheated now."

Even though my father's death was recognized by us all as the most important event of our childhood, it was not the event that defined us as persons. Rather, we each defined our father's death according to who we already were as individuals. Therefore, *it's not our childhood events that define us. It is we who define the meaning and effect of these events in our lives.* I believe that we define these events according to our own individual vantage point of reality. There is something different about each of us even before the events of childhood take place.

YOUR UNIQUENESS FROM DAY ONE

The idea of innate differences always reminds me of what parents say when they describe their children as newborns. "Chucky was as bright as a penny from the first moment." Or, "When they first put Sheila in my arms she curled up real cozily, and she's still like that now." Or, "Mikey was a handful from the start. He was wiggling all around in his nursery crib." And, "Maria was looking around with those big beautiful eyes even in the hospital that first day." Each new little baby has a curiously unique way about him or her. Whatever it is, this "way about us" seems to stay with us throughout life. I think that there is something distinct and defining about us from the very beginning. It's as though we all look at life through different glasses. If you have pink and I have blue glasses, you will see the world as pink and I will see the world as blue. How we see the world, how we feel about life, what we think about ourselves and others all depends on who we are from the very beginning of life.

This idea, that we are who we are from the beginning, fits in very well with the idea that we are all made in the image and likeness of God. We are destined to reflect God to the world. From the very beginning of your creation and minc, we each were created to be who we are. I was created by God to be me, and you were created to be you. Much has happened to each of us along the way in our lives. For example, all the people who have been a part of our lives have treated us in many different ways. And the various events of our lives have continuously provided opportunities for change and growth. Sometimes we've grown and other times we've resisted the invitations to change. We've gone forward in life and flourished. We've also held back and built defenses to cover and protect ourselves. A great deal has been added to or overlaid onto our original persons. But the original person is still there at the core regardless of what has happened to us in life. Each of us was created to be a particular image, a unique reflection of God, and this core aspect never changes. The Enneagram description of nine different types of persons simply illustrates the variety of these reflections.

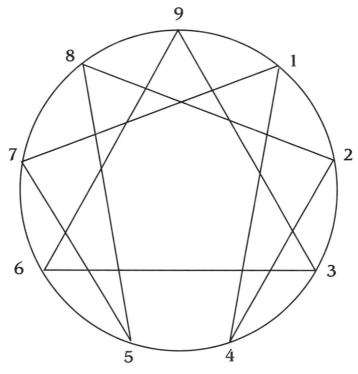

Figure One

CHAPTER THREE

Becoming Your Own Observer

RIP VAN WINKLE AND SLEEPING BEAUTY

J ust as these fabled characters once awoke from deep sleeps to embrace new lives, we too can wake up to our true selves. However, this can happen only if we open our eyes, ears, and all our senses, both interior and exterior. We have become so accustomed to ourselves with coverings over us that we don't even sense, feel, or know much of what exists underneath. It's as if we are living life on automatic pilot. We arc asleep at the wheel, but the machine keeps whirring along just as it always has.

Do you *always* react to the "obnoxious" people in your life the same way you *always* have? Do you *always* get impatient or angry with them? Or are you the type who *always* shrugs your shoulders and withdraws? Or do you *always* try to placate them? Obviously, the important word here is "always." Do you *always* do what you've *always* done? Is life a series of knee-jerk habitual reactions? If so, then you're asleep at the wheel as most of us so often are. We usually get some small glimmer of this in our mid-thirties. Then in our forties and fifties, if we haven't allowed ourselves to slip into a lifelong coma, the glimmer has grown to a loud clamor. That's the sound of the original self banging on the armored doors demanding to come out into the fresh air and sunlight.

The secret to freeing the original self is to find out from what material we have constructed the covering, our armored doors which keep the original gifted core of our beings entrapped. Since we ourselves once built the armored doors which cover the self, we must somehow, somewhere have the formula for releasing those doors. Once we recover this formula, then the doors can be opened wide to free the gifted core within us. However, this special knowledge we seek will emerge only through self-observation.

THE INNER OBSERVER

So we must each develop an Inner Observer. This is a part of ourselves which stands back from the mindless busyness of our lives and objectively observes everything about us. It simply notices our thoughts and ways of thinking, our feelings and ways of expressing, our choices of action and process of choosing, our good and poor relations with others, our spontaneous reactions, underlying attitudes and motivations. Yes, there's much to notice, isn't there? Yet all of this can be noted only if we develop an Inner Observer who remains always on duty. This idea is not meant to suggest that we stop living while we just reflect on life. Rather, we go right on the way we always have, but we watch the action of our life almost as if we were watching another person. We actually expand our focus. We remain involved with life, and we stand outside our lives at the same time.

Did you ever see an "ambiguous picture" like the one shown on the next page? (See Figure 2.) Most people viewing this see either the two faces or the vase. Try seeing both by alternating your focus quickly from the foreground to the background. The more you do it the easier it gets. This is something like what we will experience if we develop an Inner Observer. We will go about our regular lives, and we will also be observing ourselves as we think and feel and interact with life.

Figure Two

For example, as I write these ideas I'm also noticing how restless I am to get the words flowing as quickly as the ideas do. I'm noticing how tight my shoulders and fingers are getting. Oh, I just heard a fire siren. Now I hear me talking to myself: "What's your hurry? There's no fire. Loretta, slow down and relax." And then I wonder how often I'll say that to myself before I've completed this book. I love to wonder! I'm fascinated by what my Inner Observer notices.

The most important part about self-observation is to enjoy everything we discover and judge none of it. We are only trying to develop an Inner Observer which will uncover our original selves. If we begin to judge what we find, the original self will go into hiding once again. If the Inner Observer becomes a judge, it will be suspected as a dangerous intruder. So go slowly, go easily and just observe, don't judge.

THE JOURNEY AWAITS

Self-observation is an integral part of the Enneagram theory. The Enneagram can lead us on our own journey inward to the very core of our persons. However, because it is a journey, it will take time and require considerable patience. It will continually invite us to new depths of self-awareness. The Enneagram can be the guide for this journey. The fuel which propels us onward will be our own persistent curiosity about the question: Who am I? And the map which we follow will be gradually created by our own self-observation. Every time we observe ourselves, we find clues which will lead us to the next deeper level of self. Slowly but progressively we will uncover, layer by layer, the real person at the core of each of us.

YOUR SELF-OBSERVATION JOURNAL

Our logbook for the journey will be a *Self-Observation Journal* which I would like to encourage you to begin writing with this chapter. This journal will be both a record of our journey as we proceed and an invitation which moves us onward. Throughout this book, the presentation will alternate between theory and examples. The various examples offered will provide a kind of springboard for self-observation.

In creating your Journal, you may choose to write in prose or even poetry. Or your journaling may consist of lists of words, drawings, pictures, or perhaps a collage. Choose the format that feels most natural for you and one which best gets you down on paper. Create whatever will be the best style of journaling for your Enneagram journey.

Becoming Your Own Observer

Let's start the journaling process with these examples:

(1) Remember that differing views of reality produce different responses to reality. In the "cracked sidewalk" story of Chapter One, you read nine different responses to the same reality of a friend tripping on a cracked sidewalk and falling. These nine different responses reflect each of the nine positions of the Enneagram. However, these responses are only the tip of the iceberg when it comes to self-awareness. The most important information lies hidden underneath. It answers the question, "Why did each person respond the way he or she did?" *WHY* is always the most important question.

Let me suggest what each person in the "cracked sidewalk" story might say is the basic attitude beneath the response given.

The Number One person

Response: "It's inexcusable to leave a sidewalk in such poor condition."

Underlying Attitude: (Accidents happen only as a result of negligence.)

The Number Two person

Response: "Awwwh. You poor thing. Let me help you up."

Underlying Attitude: (Other people's needs are first and foremost.)

The Number Three person

Response: "Here, I'm good at that sort of thing. I'll do it."

Underlying Attitude: (Be the best at whatever you do.)

The Number Four person

Response: "I fell like this once, and I was in bed for two weeks afterwards."

Underlying Attitude: (We each are a part of each other's pain.)

The Number Five person

Response: "Isn't it interesting how everyone is reacting differently to the same event."

Underlying Attitude: (It's important to observe first in order to understand.)

The Number Six person

Response: "Are you okay? Oh gosh, now we are all going to be late. This is awful. What should we do?"

Underlying Attitude: (Be a loyal and faithful friend, but be careful because something's always likely to go wrong.)

The Number Seven person

Response: "Wow! What a fall! Hey, but you'll be up and dancing in no time."

Underlying Attitude: (Accentuate the positive!)

The Number Eight person

Response: "I'm going to get hold of the building manager and demand that this be rectified immediately."

Underlying Attitude: (Don't let anyone "get the better" of you.)

The Number Nine person

Response: "Calm down, Everyone. Everything is going to be all right. Let's not get too excited."

Underlying Attitude: (Don't let anything disturb you.)

Self-Observation: Picture yourself in the same situation. Notice how you respond and why.

Journal your response and your underlying attitude. Then notice which of the nine responses and attitudes is the most like yours.

(2) For fun, notice and record how people in your own daily life encounter the same events yet have differing reactions. Try simple examples, such as these:

    —changes in the weather,

    —missing a train or bus,

    —experiencing a tailgating driver,

    —looking forward to a social event or holiday.

(3) Try to interest your fellow workers, family members, or other friends in doing the following simple exercise.

(a) Assuming the group of persons is gathered all in one room, ask each person to focus on one very specific part of the room.

(b) Direct each one to report briefly his or her specific view of the room.

(c) Simply enjoy the variety of views reported about the same room and the different choice of words used, as well as the different manners of reporting.

(d) Journal your findings, reactions and insights.

CHAPTER FOUR

Created in the Image and Likeness of God

W hen we look in a mirror we don't see ourselves. We see only an image of ourselves. It is a reflection. In my spiritual perspective I think of each of us as created by God and living in this world as a reflection of our Creator. Of course, since this world is far from Paradise, so too is our reflection of God far from a true likeness. But we will discuss that in the next chapter. For now, let us just consider how each of the nine Enneagram views of reality may be seen as a particular reflection of God.

While the Enneagram theory is not specifically religious, it can be related to spiritual themes. This seems very useful for those who wish to view personhood from both a psychological and a spiritual perspective. My spiritual application of the Enneagram may not be the same as yours. Still I hope it will provide some added light for your journey. As I describe what I would say about each of the Numbers, let your Inner Observer notice your own reactions: your thoughts, your emotions and even your physical sensations.

THE NUMBER ONE PERSON is created to reflect the image of God as complete, perfect. The Ones have an instinct for *completion and perfection*, which permeates their whole persons. They also instinctively sense the opposite: *incompleteness and limitation*. It seems to be an inborn instinct. It's as if this sense is recorded in their DNA. A humorous but true example: Several persons I know who are Number Ones have told me of their instinctive urge to rearrange other people's office desks or kitchen cabinets. Why? "So they will be organized properly, the way they should be." Everything about the Ones senses all the parts of life as either in *completion and perfection* or *incompleteness and limitation*. Everything and everyone they encounter in life will be evaluated by this standard of measure. I often think, in a semi-facetious way, that maybe we all once lived together in Paradise. Yet, it's only the Ones among us who remember how perfect it was. The gift of the Ones will provide for the rest of us a beacon, an ideal, a model of how this world could be. They will also work tirelessly to try to bring that ideal world into reality. This innate sense that Ones have about these issues is what makes them distinctively who they are. Each of the Numbers has a distinct gift. The gift of the Number Ones is to reflect the goodness of God's perfect plan for us.

THE NUMBER TWO PERSON comes into this world reflecting God as the one who nurtures and cares for us. The Twos have a natural feel for *caring and nurturing*. They also instinctively feel the *neediness* of others and move forward to provide the needed caring. Among the Twos whom I know, what is most striking to me is how their gift moves in on needs so quickly. It's always fascinating to experience Twos entering a room in which I am waiting to meet them. They immediately say something like, "Oh dear, you've been waiting for me." Or, "Oh, come with me and we'll get you some refreshments after your long trip here." Or, "You are so kind to have made a special trip just to see me." Everything about the Number Twos, their feelings, thoughts and actions, will all be focused on the *caring and the neediness* of other people. They reflect something of God's graciousness to us.

THE NUMBER THREE PERSON brings a completely different gift which reflects God as Creator. The Creator brought about everything from nothing. Out of the void God created the world. The Number Threes reflect this by making something out of what might seem nothing to someone else. They have a keen feel for *producing or making* things happen. And they also have an instinct for recognizing when there is a lack of activity, no productivity, no-thing, the *void of nothingness*. This gift will, in one way or another, be reflected to the world in the way Threes "do" life. It will also be apparent in the way they verbalize about activity: "I'm always on the go," and "I can run with that," and "Let's get the show on the road." You can hear production in motion when you listen to them speak. Their gift is to reflect God's great hope in us. The Threes reflect for us how promising we are, especially if we are open to God's creative plan for us.

THE NUMBER FOUR PERSON comes into the world to reflect what we think of as the uniqueness of God. Monotheism, the belief that there is only one God, came into this world with the Jewish tradition of faith. Yahweh means "I Am Who Am." This uniqueness signifies that there is only one of a kind, one God. Each one of us is likewise one of a kind. The Number Fours have a special sensitivity for this *uniqueness*. They also have a feeling for the opposite: *commonness*. They tend to appreciate each person and life itself as unique. They also feel a painful aversion for common ordinariness. This is their gift. You can be sure that the Fours in your life are not like anyone else. They will present themselves differently. They see and explain life differently. And, strange as it may sound, they wish they didn't feel differently than others do. It can be very painful. Yet this is also their gift. The Fours offer to the rest of us someone who will share in our pain and our sufferings. They reflect God's sensitivity to our human uniqueness.

THE NUMBER FIVE PERSON reflects to the world the gift of knowing. One image we commonly have of God is that of the All-knowing. Of course, the Number Fives are not all-knowing. However, their particular gift is an instinctive knowledge about *knowing and not knowing*. The Fives have a special perspective about knowing. It's almost like having a panoramic view of the countryside. They see life as a continuous process which invites us to go farther and farther in the discovery of truth. It's a gradual journey that can only be taken one step at a time. However, each new step builds on a former step. It's a journey of life and growth processes. The Fives see every moment in this process as an opportunity to learn. This is the main focus of all their activities. Their gift is to be open to learning, and available to us when we choose to learn alongside them. The Fives reflect God's understanding acceptance of us humans as beings in process, on our way home.

THE NUMBER SIX PERSON reflects to the world the gift of faith. In the Old Testament we read about a very strong image of God. "I will be your God and you will be my people." This same bond of God's faithfulness is also in the New Testament. "I will be with you always." There is in these promises a sense of faithfulness, fidelity and certainty. It is the Number Sixes who reflect to the world a knowledge of this bond of faith. They know and understand the concept of *faith*, as well as the discomfort of the opposite: *uncertainty*. The Sixes know that all of us are bonded with each other in the human family. We all belong to each other. We are and always will be sisters and brothers in one family. It is this sense of belonging to the human family which the Sixes offer to others. They reach out to welcome all the newcomers who seem uncertain or insecure. They offer to others trust and reliability in friendship. They seem able to be committed to others through all the ups and downs of relating. The Sixes reflect God's faith that we can and will "bear each other's burdens and share each other's joys."

THE NUMBER SEVEN PERSON reflects to the world the great gift of joy. In the book of *Genesis*, God looks upon all that has been created and pronounces: "It is very good." The Number Sevens say this about everything: "It is very good, great, wonderful, fantastic, terrific!" The Sevens know and experience *joy* and delight. They also know about *sadness*, pain and sorrow. You may not see this in the Sevens, but they are keenly aware of pain and sorrow. They somehow know that true joy is born from accepting pain as a necessary part of the process of growth. For those who are in pain, Sevens offer the promise of new life. When happiness abounds they delight in it. When sadness occurs they will "look for the silver lining" or "make lemonade from the lemon." Their gift is a knowledge that the heights of true joy are scaled from the depths of sadness. The Sevens reflect God's utter delight with us in each moment of our journey.

THE NUMBER EIGHT PERSON reflects that attribute of God which we call "All-powerful." The Eights have a strong sense of *power* and its effects. All they do in the world will somehow be based on this power issue. They sense how power can be used for both good and evil. They likewise have an almost infallible sense of the opposite: *vulnerability and weakness*. They can be fearless and bold in confronting evil and injustice. The Eights will use their power to protect the weak and downtrodden. They show little hesitation in uncovering pretense. The Eights have in them an instinctive sense that power can create new life. This power of the Eight is like what we witness in political revolutions and in the eruption of volcanoes. Both result in massive changes and new beginnings. It is also like the tremendous force involved in childbirth which results in the birth of a new and fragile person in this world. The Eights reflect for us the majestic power and the tender mercies of God.

THE NUMBER NINE PERSON comes into the world reflecting that attribute of God which we think of as harmonious and unifying. The Number Nines try to bring everything and everyone together in peace. They have a strong instinct for *harmony* and likewise have a particular sense for *discord*. They relate to the world, other people and even themselves from this viewpoint of harmony and discord. They have the patience and endurance to support others through experiences of personal turmoil. The Nines are also good at building bridges to bring together people who seem otherwise locked into some kind of disagreement with each other. The Nines will search for and work toward conflict resolutions and peaceful outcomes. Their sense of discord helps them to know just what might be done to bring about a union of opposites. Their own non-judgmental approach encourages forgiveness among disputing individuals and compromise between groups. Nines believe that within each person's heart is a love for all others. Yet they realize that peace is woven from many disparate and conflicting elements. Their gift reflects to the world the God of peace.

When we combine all these gifts together, of course, we don't really approach the fullness of God. We are not God and we never will be. But we can exhibit some reflection of God to each other. The Enneagram has a way of helping us get in touch with our God-given giftedness. It can be a wonderful help for what I think of as our life-journey. The Enneagram can help us to discover our own basic gifts that have existed in each of us from the first moment of life. Once we have made this discovery, we can allow these God-given, God-reflecting gifts to develop within us. And finally, we can freely offer our gifts to one another. In making this discovery and allowing this growth, we would provide a wonderful reflection of God in this world of ours. We would then have a greater sense of our communal giftedness and some grasp of the fullness of God.

SELF-OBSERVATION JOURNAL:
When you think about these nine different gifts which were described, how do you see yourself in relation to them? Is there one, or perhaps two or three, that sounded like your giftedness? Record in your journal, in some way, your self-observation at this point regarding your personal giftedness. (See Figure Three on next page.)

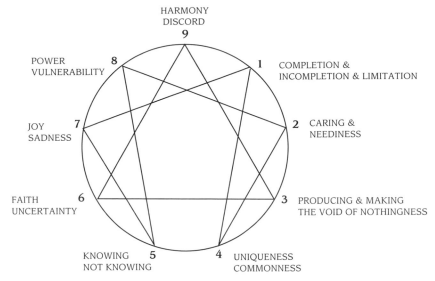

HARMONY
DISCORD
9

POWER
VULNERABILITY   8

1   COMPLETION &
INCOMPLETION & LIMITATION

JOY   7
SADNESS

2   CARING &
NEEDINESS

FAITH   6
UNCERTAINTY

3   PRODUCING & MAKING
THE VOID OF NOTHINGNESS

KNOWING   5
NOT KNOWING

4   UNIQUENESS
COMMONNESS

Figure Three

CHAPTER FIVE

From Our Royal Infancy Years Onward

FAIRY TALES MAY BE TRUE

Once upon a time there were triplets born into the world. They were born in a very beautiful place where the weather was ideal and food was plentiful. Their parents and several adult relatives were delighted to be on hand to care for them in every way they might need. Whenever the triplets even looked like they wanted to eat, someone would be at their sides immediately to feed them. As the infants grew into toddlers, their lives continued to be very happy.

Then one day the triplets noticed that the sky had grown dark, the wind began blowing cold and strong, and suddenly all the adults were nowhere to be found.

SELF-OBSERVATION JOURNAL: Stop for a moment. How would you react if you were one of the triplets, when "the big people" left you?

To continue . . . The triplets began to ask one another about what was happening to them and more importantly why. The *first* of the triplets said: "My opinion is that we must have done something wrong. All the big people have judged us as bad so they have cut us off from them and from all that we need for survival. It makes me really angry that they would do this to us. It isn't fair. I'm going to take charge of myself from now on like they do themselves. If they ever come back, I'll never let them treat me as a little weakling again. I'll keep control. I'll show them. I'll be as strong as they are. Then maybe someday they will realize again that I'm good."

The *second* triplet said: "I feel really disheartened about all that's happening. The big people must not like us any more. They probably think we're ugly or defective in some way. It makes me feel so anxious to be alone and rejected like this. I'm going to make myself into a very pleasing person in every way. Then I hope everyone else who meets me from now on will like me and not reject me. I'll never let those who have rejected me know how hurt I feel. But if I'm attractive and accomplished enough, maybe someday even the big people will want to be with me again."

The *third* triplet said: "I think there must be a logical reason why all this is happening. I think the big people have gone away and abandoned us because we were little people. We were lacking in some way. It's very scary to be left like this without knowing what to do. I'm going to have to figure out everything by myself now. Maybe if I learn enough about life and people, then no one else I meet will ever think of me as lacking in any way. Instead they'll see me as someone who is knowledgeable and sure of myself. If I see the big people again, I won't let them know what I don't know. If they think I know what I'm doing, maybe they will want to join me again. And, maybe I'll let them. We'll see."

SELF-OBSERVATION JOURNAL: Stop now and record your thoughts on which of the triplets reacted most like you would have to the disappearance of "the big people."

FROM PARADISE TO THE HUMAN CONDITION

Even though this story is obviously written as a fairy tale, it probably is close to what we felt like in the years before we could speak and understand language. In those first few years of life, we had a lot of rude awakenings. From the first time food or comfort did not arrive on command from us, we suffered a loss. One shocking disappointment after another brought the message home more and more clearly. All too suddenly we found out that this was not Paradise and we were not the reigning royalty.

What had happened to this wonderful world God made? What about these beautiful gifts we were each to bring into the world? If we were all so beautifully gifted, if we were meant to be valuable contributors to this world, why don't we act more like it? Why don't we treat each other more like gifts? These are, of course, age-old questions. And everyone has a different way of answering them. The world of theology talks about "the fall from grace" and its effects. In the field of psychology, it is said that the events of our childhood tend to limit our potential. G.K. Chesterton once described our human understanding of the world as a miracle, but something went wrong with it. Something has been lost along the way. Most of us recognize this as the human condition. The world is somehow less than we wish it was, and so are we. Then what did happen to the original gifts? And what happened to us in early life? Most importantly, can our original gifts be retrieved at all?

ADAPTING TO THE BOGEYMAN

The following is an explanation drawn from psychology, spirituality and the Enneagram. The first loss we suffered set off a signal which began our adaptation process. In fact, from the very first moments of our existence and consequently all through life, we have been "adapting." What we are adapting to is not merely little inconveniences. We're not just adapting to not receiving a fresh, new baby bottle when we were infants or to not getting a parking place as adults. It is a much larger issue than these things. All these smaller deprivations activate in us a core fear that we could actually be deprived of life. They painfully remind us of our mortality.

In other words, we all have a basic fear of death, of ceasing to exist. We all fear that something we say or do may cause others to cut us off, to reject us, or to abandon us. Then we would be all alone. Just like in the little children's game of Farmer in the Dell, none of us wants to be in the middle all by ourselves hearing the last line of the rhyme: "And the cheese stands alone." When this realization comes to us as young children, it comes as a threat to our very survival. We instinctively respond by adapting to the powers-that-be so that we can be guaranteed a continuation of survival, connection and inclusion in the human family.

What we each decide to call this life-threatening danger will be different from one Enneagram position to the next. As children we usually called it the bogeyman or a monster. In adulthood we have more sophisticated ways of referring to this basic fear. We speak of "separation anxiety," "rejection complexes," or "abandonment issues." The sense that there is some basic danger to be feared is very much a part of our human instinctual life. Curiously, so is the adaptation process we employ to protect us from the danger.

BUILDING OUR PROTECTIVE COVERS

As we adapt we build walls, clothe ourselves in armor and carry weapons of self-defense. We cover ourselves to protect us from the danger. Just as we have different names for the danger, we also have different walls, armor and weapons. Both the danger and the defenses are identified by each Enneagram number according to each particular view of reality.

For example, the Number Twos will feel that the danger arises from neglect. The Number Fives will view the danger within the context of knowing and not knowing. The Number Eights will sense the danger as a power issue. The particular defenses chosen will follow from the dangers identified. The Two will create a wall which seems to be built of caring but is actually an adapted version of the original gift. The Five will construct a wall of knowledge which mimics the original gift of knowing. The Eight will have a self-styled wall which resembles the original gift of power, and so forth. We will cover our fearful selves with adaptations of the original God-gifted selves.

WE COVER OURSELVES WITH "OURSELVES"

It's something like when a little child has finished taking a bath and comes running into the living room in nothing but bare skin. The child is as proud as can be and shouts with glee: "Look at my clean little body! Isn't is nice?" Then the little child looks up and sees us. We are strangers to the child. Instinctively the little one senses danger in this happening. Oftentimes what children do in such situations is cover themselves with themselves. They fold their arms and legs around the trunks of their bodies as if to hide and protect themselves from the supposed danger.

We do something similar throughout life, from childhood through adulthood. Whenever we sense danger we conclude that there is something wrong, defective or lacking in us. Then we instinctively move to cover ourselves with ourselves. We each make an adapted version of our original self. We make a copy of the basic quality of our original gifts and use this to cover ourselves. We then claim to have created ourselves. We cover our real selves with an adapted version of ourselves. The cover is our persona or personality, not our real selves. Although this cover looks real, it actually is a self-made version of the original God-given gift. It's not bad; it's just not real. In any case, we claim the credit. For example, the Number One person overdevelops the capacity to improve everyone and everything that is encountered. Then we hear this same Number One say: "I have made myself perfect. I made you perfect. I made this event perfect. Therefore, I am perfect!" In psychology this is referred to as the "ego" talking, not the true self.

LOSING TOUCH WITH OUR ORIGINAL SELVES

What happens to us in this adaptation process is very much like the following example. If we were to plant a rosebush or another species of delicate plant, we would have to put something around it, like chicken wire. We have to provide protection from small animals who might damage the plant. Maybe we even have to cover the wire with burlap to keep the wind from blowing it down or to protect it from the digging of squirrels. All we do is meant to protect it, to protect our original rosebush. However, if after the rosebush begins to grow and flourish, we don't take away our burlap covers, we might only be able to say: "I have a burlap bush in the backyard" (instead of a rosebush). And that is something like what happens to us as we go through life. We begin to think of and talk about the cover we have put on to protect us as though it were actually our true selves. We don't talk about the original gift, which is the God-given gift.

So, in the process, we really lose touch with ourselves. We identify with the false covering, the false self. It initially was instinctual to cover ourselves, the basic instinct of self-preservation. If we hadn't covered ourselves physically and psychologically in this world, we would not have been able to survive. It was necessary for us to develop this covering. It is important to know this so that we can have true compassion for ourselves. However, as adults, we may no longer need the covering. Yet we still hold on to it and even boast about it. We say: "I am the cover." We forget that God made the original. We probably no longer need the cover, the wall, the armor and defense mechanisms. However, we have fallen asleep to reality and become so accustomed to the cover that we think it's the real thing. We need instead to find a way to shed our cover, to let go of our ego, to retrieve our original God-gifted selves, to discover the lost treasure of our true persons.

CHAPTER SIX

The Three Enneagram Centers

THE THREE CENTERS OF BEING

We will each eventually find ourselves as one of the nine Numbers. When we do, we will also find out that we are part of one of three Centers. Or we may find our Center first and only then our individual Number. What significance does the Center have for us? Gurdjieff's most original contribution to the Enneagram teaching was in regard to these three Centers. He taught that we are actually "three-brained beings." What is meant by this is that we each have three centers of intelligence, three faculties through which we can know ourselves, others and the world. (See Illustration on next page.)

We humans can know and understand reality through the use of our heads (The Cognitive Center), through our hearts (The Emotion-Motion Center) and through the experience of our bodies (The Gut-Instinct Center). Each of these three Centers includes three Enneagram Numbers. However, one of these "learning centers" will be the most dominant of the three for each of us. And, whatever is our most dominant Center will also be the most developed.

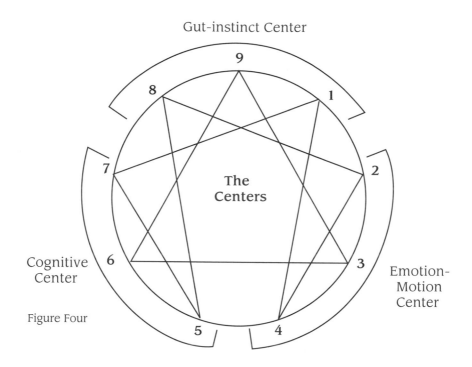

Gut-instinct Center

The Centers

Cognitive Center

Emotion-Motion Center

Figure Four

In fact, we will eventually find that it is over-developed. We tend to overdue that at which we are best. Consequently, the Centers other than our own will be underdeveloped. After we have found our Numbers and then begin to look at the possibilities for further growth, we can begin to consider how to balance our use of the three Centers more evenly. For now, it is enough to know that each of us is one of the Numbers in one of these three Centers. For many of us it's hard to identify our Number among the nine. A good place to start is to locate ourselves in one of the three Centers first, if that's possible.

THE TRIPLETS AND THE THREE ENNEAGRAM CENTERS

Remember the triplets from Chapter Five? They seem to have been born into a kind of Paradise where everyone else served their needs. Then suddenly the triplets were left alone to fend for themselves. Each one of the triplets reacted to this in a different way. Now let's use the same triplet story to examine the three Centers of being. Each triplet represents a different one of the three Centers. Let's take a closer look at their reactions to see how they relate to the three Centers. Keep your Inner Observer in active gear so you can compare your own reactions to the descriptions that follow. Notice which of the triplets' reactions seem to be most like what your reactions might be in a similar situation. This could help you find your Center and maybe even your Number.

THE FIRST TRIPLET REPRESENTS THE GUT-INSTINCT CENTER

When "the big people" left, the first triplet:

> sensed a threat to survival,
> was immediately angry,
> concluded the triplets themselves had been
> judged "bad" and therefore had been cut off
> (separated) by the adults.

So this first triplet resolved to take charge, hold firm, keep control, in general be as strong as possible. This represents what the Numbers in the Gut-Instinct Center will do.

THE SIMILARITIES AMONG THE EIGHT-NINE-ONE PERSONS

The first triplet's reactions, just described here, are the same as the basic reactions that emerge from the underlying motivations of the Enneagram Numbers Eight, Nine and One. These three Numbers are all in the Gut-Instinct Center. To all these three types of persons, the dangers that threaten them in life are always interpreted as "survival" issues. The threat is that others may force them to move against their wills. Only when these persons have a sense of being in charge of themselves, without control from others, do they feel secure.

Whenever a threat is sensed by the Eights, Nines or Ones:

> The emotional reaction is immediate anger.
> The assumed conclusion is: I am bad and, therefore, unacceptable.
> The perceived result of the "badness" is to be cut off or separated.
> The cover each of these Numbers will create for protection will present the impression of strength, resolve and control.

THE DIFFERENCES AMONG THE EIGHT-NINE-ONE PERSONS

Though the Eights, Nines and Ones all have some things in common, they differ in the way they present themselves. Regarding the emotional expression of *anger,* Eights will be forthright in their expression. They may just wipe you away by debunking what you've said. Or they will shout and stomp, leaving you no doubt that they are angry. The Nines' anger will be indirect and passively aggressive. They may channel the energy of their anger into trying to calm everyone down and smooth things over. Or, they will appear to shut down their considerable force and figuratively sit down right in the path of forward motion. *You* might be very angry, but *they* will seem to have done nothing but stop. Have you ever been walking directly behind someone when they suddenly stop? You, too, are stopped cold as you bump into them. This is how it can feel when relating to an angry Nine. The Ones, however, will repress their anger beneath a tense and rigid emotional and physical control. They may criticize, scold or even reprimand others. Or they may simply smile with their jaws clenched, while they suck in the anger with a deep breath. They may vehemently deny that they are angry, but it sure feels like there's anger permeating the whole atmosphere.

As to their conclusion that they have been judged as bad, the Eights will pretend to revel in their "badness." Their behavioral response will seem to say: "You better believe I'm a handful. What's more I'll give you another handful to try to cope with, so there!" The Nines will accept the verdict of "badness" with depressed resignation as if they had expected it. "Nobody ever cares about what I think anyway. It's no big deal." However, the Ones will show an externally cowering look while seething internally with resentment. "I was only trying to be helpful."(Inside: How dare you criticize me!)

When the Eights perceive that they have been *cut off or separated* because of their supposed badness, they will express outrage at the cut-off, and they will push for justice or revenge: "You can't fire me. I quit." The Nines will ignore the cut-off or pretend they don't care while they smolder in a quiet withdrawal. "It makes no difference to me." (Silently: You creep!) The Ones will protest their blamelessness and reprimand their accusers. "I was trying so hard. I meant well. I've gotten better though, haven't I? Besides, you're wrong. I wasn't angry."

THE GUT-INSTINCT CENTER

The three Numbers, Eight-Nine-One, were all represented by the first triplet. These Numbers at the top of the Enneagram circle derive most of their life energy from their instincts. For all of them, their most predominant center of learning, relating and reacting is the Center of Gut-Instinct. When their instincts move them, they are immediately and forcefully in action. They will push for peace and justice and what they sense is right. If you ask them why they're doing whatever they're doing, they often can't explain. "Why?" is a head question, and the action they took did not come through the head but rather from their instinctive sense. In describing the energy of the Eight-Nine-One group, I like to use the autonomic nervous system as a bodily symbol to represent the same reflexive action of these three. For example, when the doctor taps your knee with the little reflex hammer and your lower leg jerks forward, that is similar to the immediate energy that is most active in the Eight-Nine-One persons. These are people whom we might refer to as "mid-brain" people. The mid-brain is the part of our brains which regulates the instinctive reactions, mainly those of self-preservation.

These three types of persons, the Eights, Nines and Ones, relate most strongly to the environment. Their mental process of dealing with the facts of reality is one of making judgments about people and issues by comparing good versus bad, right versus wrong, and so forth. They simply "instinctively know." They either like or dislike someone or something immediately. Another good physical symbol for this group might be the body's alimentary system which takes in food, assimilates some, and then eliminates the rest to preserve the life of the body. This system is continually "sorting out" what is good from what is bad or toxic. It seeks to keep what is good and discard what is bad. This bodily process is similar to how the Eight-Nine-One persons relate to the world. They see life as a struggle to survive. They are attracted to the good and seek to eliminate the bad.

The Eight-Nine-One persons are also analogical thinkers. They often use examples or stories, similes and metaphors to explain their thoughts, like the use of the triplet story in these chapters. Oftentimes when asked how they feel, they will answer by saying: "It's like the time when I. . . ." As you listen to this story from their past experience, they seem to be saying that the feeling they had at this earlier time is somehow similar to the way they feel now. Consequently, the Eight-Nine-One persons learn best through stories and bodily experiences. They often report hating school but loving recess and sports. Regardless of how intelligent they may be, for persons of this center, learning takes place through the gut-instinct, physical center of their beings. And, sadly, beyond the level of kindergarten, most opportunities to learn kinesthetically or bodily have been filtered out of the school experience. These people are grounded in the world of matter. They can be very frugal with their material possessions and are often "territorial" about their space. In manner we are likely to find the Eights direct and forthright, the Nines settled and unpretentious, and the Ones controlled and precise.

THE SECOND TRIPLET REPRESENTS
THE EMOTION-MOTION CENTER

When "the big people" left, the second triplet:

> felt disconnected and alone,
> felt depressed, anxious and hurt,
> decided the triplets must have been seen as
> ugly or defective and therefore were rejected
> by the adults.

So this second triplet was persuaded to become helpful, accomplished and attractive in order to be likable. This represents what the Numbers in the Emotion-Motion Center will do.

THE SIMILARITIES AMONG THE
TWO-THREE-FOUR PERSONS

The second triplet's reactions, just described here, are the same as the basic reactions that emerge from the underlying motivations of the Enneagram Numbers Two, Three and Four. These three Numbers are all in the Emotion-Motion Center. All of these three types of persons consistently interpret the dangers that threaten them in terms of possible disconnection. Survival among these persons is based on a feeling of "social" security. They feel secure whenever they are accepted, liked by or connected to others.

> Whenever a threat is felt by the Twos, Threes or Fours:
> The emotional reaction is anxiety or depression.
> The assumed conclusion is: I am defective and, therefore, unacceptable.
> The perceived result of "defectiveness" is rejection.
> The cover each of these Numbers will create for protection will be appealing, attractive, and it will display accomplishment.

THE DIFFERENCES AMONG THE TWO-THREE-FOUR PERSONS

Though similar in their basic orientation, these three types of persons show a nuanced difference one from another. The emotional expression of *anxiety or depression* by the Twos is usually quite open and expressive. However, it is typically focused on someone else and is often positive. For example, if Twos feel depressed they may tap into our sadness instead of their own. "It must be so hard to do all you do for others with no thanks from them." Or if Twos are anxious about whether or not they are valued by others, they may compliment those others. "You always do such wonderful things for people." The Twos take care of you in hopes that you will take care of them. The Threes will channel their anxiety into activity. And they will work to escape from depression by setting new goals requiring even more activity. If this doesn't work, they will try to make a project out of the time between projects. They are not in depression, just "on hiatus between jobs" or they are "busy regrouping." Although the Threes sometimes talk about their emotions, we rarely feel these emotions in them. With the Fours we will surely feel wave after wave of undulating emotion churning within them. Sometimes we will also experience it fluttering around them in anxious moments. Their emotions may be communicated through gestures, symbols or impressions. However, they will most likely not be expressed in any direct way.

The sense of *defectiveness* that the Two-Three-Four persons share in common will also feel different in each of these Numbers. The Twos will feel angry at whoever they assume has deemed them defective, but they will also feel guilt about the anger. The Threes will not accept the label outwardly but rather reframe it so that it feels like positive feedback to them. Yet somewhere within them, they will shudder at the possibility that they may very well be defective or inadequate. The Fours will fully claim the defectiveness internally while lamenting their sorry state. Yet in public they will carry on in a very poised way.

The perceived *rejection* as a result of "defectiveness" will cause the Twos to try to activate guilt in whoever they feel has rejected them: "How could you do this to me after all I've done for you?" With a flair of positivity, the Threes will thank you for being so open with them. "Thank you for your sharing. The best thing for me about hearing this is to know you could open up to me. This is a good learning experience. It's something I can build on. I can take it and run with it." And they *will* run to any next place where they will be loved anew. The Fours will keep their composure externally but internally sink deeply into a familiar emotional state of depressed anguish at their defectiveness.

THE EMOTION-MOTION CENTER

The second triplet has given us a glimpse of some underlying themes common to the Two-Three-Four persons. These three Numbers grouped at the right side of the Enneagram circle share the center most focused on motion which follows from emotion. For example, when the Twos feel lonely they will go in search of someone to companion. When the Threes feel depressed they set a new goal and start the activity that will soon accomplish it. When the Fours feel ugly they might spend time, energy and money creating something beautiful: a special room, a garden, a book of poetry, a new fashion look. The circulatory system is a good bodily symbol to represent the continual motion and emotional energy of this group. Just as blood constantly courses through our bodies, so constant activity courses through these people continually. The Two-Three-Four persons might be referred to as "right-brain" people. This is the part of our brain which regulates emotions and creativity.

The strongest connection for these people is to others. Their deepest instinctual energy is social. They seek to quell their anxiety by connecting with others, one to one, in small groups and by building community. There is also a relational focus on image and identity. They indirectly seek feedback from others on how they are coming across publicly, how they're doing and just who others think they are. This is how they go about establishing a sense of their own identity. They consider life to be about people-connecting and task-doing. More than the other two groups, these people truly "do" life.

The Twos do for people. The Threes do projects. The Fours do something distinctive and unique.

With the same intensity that the Eight-Nine-One persons are attracted to *good*, the Two-Three-Four persons seem most attracted to *beauty*: in people, in their surroundings, and in all of life. The Two-Three-Four persons learn best by listening. So, both traditional school instruction and this present age of the media seem best suited to their learning style. They are analytic and deductive reasoners. They make general assumptions and move to particular examples. For example: "Clothing stores are patronized mostly by women, so women must love to shop. You're a woman, so I assume you love to shop." We will most likely experience the Twos as emotionally warm and intimate, the Threes as energetic and confident, and the Fours as introspective and aesthetic.

THE THIRD TRIPLET REPRESENTS
THE COGNITIVE CENTER

When "the big people" left, the third triplet:

> thought there was a logical reason for their departure,
>
> still felt fearful to be left without knowing what to do,
>
> concluded that the triplets were lacking in some way and therefore were abandoned by the adults.

So the third triplet became committed to learning all about life so as to figure out how to live. This represents what the Numbers in the Cognitive Center will do.

THE SIMILARITIES AMONG
FIVE-SIX-SEVEN PERSONS

The third triplet's reactions, just described here, are the same as the basic reactions that emerge from the underlying motivations of the Enneagram Numbers Five, Six and Seven. These three Numbers are all in the Cognitive Center. These three types of persons have always interpreted the dangers that threaten them as being left out or left in the dark, not knowing what's happening. Survival for the Five-Six-Seven persons is based on feeling safe and secure, either emotionally or physically, within their environment. If they know what's happening, they can figure out life. Then they can join in and feel secure in belonging.

Whenever a threat is perceived by the Fives, Sixes or Sevens:

> The emotional reaction is fear.
> The assumed conclusion is: I am lacking in some important way and therefore am unacceptable.
> The perceived result of "being found lacking" is abandonment.
> The cover each will create for protection will demonstrate to others that these people know what is going on and what they're doing.

THE DIFFERENCES AMONG THE
FIVE-SIX-SEVEN PERSONS

As we have seen before with the Numbers in the other two Centers, these three are similar in the basics yet different in the particular expression. The Fives register their *fear* by becoming very quiet and observant. They have a way of looking like they are still in the room and still in the conversation, while actually they have left. Their emotions are drawn away to a safe hiding place. And their minds are in another world of observation and reflection. Only their bodies are present, but they show little movement or emotional display. In psychological assessments, this is the blank face and motionless body we label as "low affect."

Others may read the Fives in an admirable way as being very self-contained, self-possessed and self-assured, but this is exactly when they are actually most afraid. The Sixes usually express this fear by fretfully seeking certainty from others' guidance. They may call out: "Oh dear, what do you think I should do?" Or, if fear threatens to become too great, they may forcefully state any certainty just to end the fear: "That's it. I've decided. Case closed." The Sevens show only exuberant enthusiasm on the outside while internally feeling fear at the level of panic or terror. The Sevens may be the life of the party. However, when they are home alone later that night, they may pace the floor with panic attacks about whatever they have to fear in life. Notice that none of these three types of persons actually expresses emotion openly, but rather, they show it in their behaviors.

The belief that something is *lacking* suggests that these people think that they are not bad or defective like the other groupings. Rather, there's just not enough to them. The Fives think they don't know enough. The Sixes worry that they're not certain enough, while the Sevens go into a panic because they might not be happy enough.

The thought of *abandonment* will cause the Fives to hold back from engagement. They will stand on the edge of the dance floor. Nothing ventured, nothing lost. The threat of abandonment keeps Sixes always on the lookout for the slightest clue of an ever-lurking something that might go wrong. If they're ready for it, they can move away from it before it moves away and abandons them first. They have an ever-present eye for danger. Sixes are often in an approach-avoidance hesitation-waltz with people. For Sevens the thought of abandonment keeps them dancing as fast as they can to keep the good times rolling and the audience applauding.

THE COGNITIVE CENTER

The third triplet, of course, represents the Five-Six-Seven persons. These three Numbers, found on the left side of the Enneagram circle, specialize in thinking. It is the most highly developed part of their persons. The Fives think so much and so intensely that they even think about their thinking process. The Sixes think in a worrisome way of all that could go wrong, and all the concerns and demands that need to be met, and of all the things that have to be prepared lest tragedy strike. The Sevens use their thinking to plan numerous options so that they do not ever feel trapped. Life must be guaranteed to remain fun and free and, therefore, safe for them. A good bodily symbol to represent the Cognitive Center is the central nervous system. These three types of people operate in the same way. All human beings collect data through the senses. However, these people are constantly collecting and fitting all this data into orderly systems through their busy mental processes. They are what might be called "left-brain" people. This is the side of the brain which regulates language concepts and logical thinking.

As you can tell, for the Five-Six-Seven persons the greatest involvement is with their thoughts and ideas. They use the activity of the head to calm their fears. The focus of their energies is always on the need and desire to know. It's a matter of survival for them. They are seeking emotional and physical safety. They have a strong instinct for "syntony," a one-to-one fitting together. Fives, Sixes and Sevens like to take ideas and create whole systems with them. Or we might also say, they enjoy taking many ideas and synthesizing them into one construct. At times their cognitive energy can even reach the level of suspicion as to others' motives. For the Five-Six-Seven persons, life is a puzzle to be figured out or solved. They plan, order and systematize in order to be safe in the world. As The Gut-Instinct Center is attracted to the *good* and the Emotion-Motion Center is attracted to *beauty*, so this Cognitive Center avidly seeks the *truth*, the facts of life.

The Five-Six-Seven persons, by contrast to the others, are inductive reasoners. They move from the particular to the general. In other words, they count all the noses and only then draw their conclusions. For example: "We are counting everyone who goes into this clothing store today so that we can establish the facts about how many men and how many women shopped in this one store on this same day. Tomorrow we will look at another store. Finally, we will assess how much of the general population is involved in shopping at certain stores on certain days of the week." The Fives, Sixes and Sevens are the true researchers. They learn best through seeing and are avid observers of their surroundings. The Fives stare, the Sixes take darting glances, and the Sevens quickly absorb everything in one smooth scan of delight. With all this mental activity they may seem to be without feelings. However, their feelings are very much alive and even accessible. It's just that they are hidden deep within them as safely buried treasure. In manner we will find that the Fives are quiet and observant. The Sixes are friendly and cautious. The Sevens are lively and entertaining.

SELF-OBSERVATION JOURNAL:

(1) The following list is a summary of all that has been described in this chapter about the three Centers. It may help you locate your Center if you look over these three columns.

THE THREE ENNEAGRAM CENTERS

	8 – 9 – 1	2 – 3 – 4	5 – 6 – 7
PERCEIVED THREAT TO:	Self-Preservation	Social Security	Physical Safety
BASIC EMOTION:	Anger	Anxiety/Depression	Fear
EXPRESSION OF EMOTION:	8: debunk 9: negate 1: scold	2: focus on others 3: into action 4: symbolize	5: observe 6: fret/dogmatic 7: fly/panic
CAUSE OF LOSS:	"Badness"	"Defectiveness"	Fear
REACTION	8: Revel in it 9: Resigned to it 1: Resent it	2: Anger/Guilt 3: Positive reframe 4: Sink into it	5: observe 6: fret/dogmatic 7: fly/panic
RESULT OF LOSS	Separation	Rejection	"Found Lacking"

	8 – 9 – 1	2 – 3 – 4	5 – 6 – 7
REACTION	8: Outrage 9: Smolder 1: Accuse	2: Instill guilt 3: Offer gratitude 4: Keep Composed	5: Question self 6: Self-doubt 7: Get frantic
COVER	8: Strength 9: Resolve 1: Control	2: Helpful 3: Accomplished 4: Attractive	5: Hold back 6: Prep for danger 7: Leap Forward
LIFE ENERGY:	Instinctively active	Body-busy	Mentally intense
DIRECTION OF ENERGY:	From instinct into action	From emotion into motion	From ideas into systems
BODILY SYMBOL:	Automatic Nervous System Alimentary System	Circulatory System	Central Nervous System
"BRAIN:"	Mid-brain	Right brain	Left brain
RELATES MOST TO:	Environment	People	Ideas
FOCUS OF RELATING:	Compare/Judge	Connect/Image	Syntony+1:1 fitting
ATTRACTION TO :	Goodness	Beauty	Truth
AVERSION FROM:	Badness	Ugliness	Falsehood
REASONING STYLE	Analogical	Deductive	Inductive
LEARNING STYLE:	Experiencing	Listening	Seeing
EMOTIONAL EXPRESSION:	Forceful/Direct	Spontaneous	Deeply hidden
FUNCTIONING STYLE:	Strategic	Practical	Systematic
IN MANNER:	8: Direct and forthright 9: Settled and Unpretentious 1: Controlled and precise	2: Emotionally warm, intimate 3:Energetic and confident 4: Introspective and aesthetic	5: Quiet and observant 6: Friendly and cautious 7: Lively and entertaining
LIFE IS A . . .	Struggle to survive or win	Series of vital things to do.	Puzzle or problem solve

(2) Imagine yourself being in the following physically and emotionally threatening situation:

You are driving your car through an intersection when suddenly another car hits your car broadside. You are alive and relatively O.K.

How would you react: What's your strongest emotion? What do you think/feel/sense about what is happening? What would you do in this situation?

(3) With which of the three Enneagram groupings do you identify the most? In which center do you think you belong: The Gut-instinct Center, The Emotion-Motion Center or The Cognitive Center? Try to locate yourself in one of the Centers by comparing the examples given throughout this chapter with your own reactions to everyday situations.

CHAPTER SEVEN

Our Idealized Self-Images

DANGER COMES IN MANY FORMS

In our discussion so far we have been talking about dangers and threats. The word *danger* usually makes us think of physical danger. Yet it is far more common for us to experience emotional or psychological danger. Usually we feel this type of danger if there is some kind of an attack on our self-image. Basically, this will happen whenever anyone challenges who we are or how we value ourselves. These attacks come in many forms, such as: being reprimanded, neglected, devalued, misunderstood, embarrassed, blamed, discouraged, belittled, ignored, and so forth. Sometimes we are actually treated in these ways. At other times it's only our interpretation of what someone has said or done. Whatever these attacks are called, real or imaginary, they always convey the same meaning: You are unacceptable as you are.

SELF-CREATING OUR COVERS

In our wounded state, we promise ourselves that we will remedy the situation so this kind of attack will never happen again. So if we experience a reprimand, we will try even harder to be above all reproach. If we feel devalued, we will work even harder to be esteemed. And if we think we have been blamed, we will be sure to be the most cooperative we can be. We will each do whatever we have to do in order to avoid future damage to our self-image. This is how we self-create the cover to protect our original God-gifted selves which seem too fragile for this world.

This cover we develop will bear only a distorted resemblance to one single part of the original gift. We self-create our interpretation of one part of the God-gift. Then we overdevelop it so that we can defend ourselves against all possible attacks. As was mentioned earlier, psychology gives this imitation or *false self* the term *persona* or *personality*. It is our *idealized self-image.* This is our overblown, out of reality, image of ourselves. It will be, of course, impossible to attain this ideal self. That would be beyond the realm of human capability. However, we will try our hardest to do so anyway. It is in the developing and maintaining of the idealized self-image that we become perfectionists. What we idealize is a certain quality. Then we convince ourselves that we must always represent a perfect portrayal of that quality. Of course, we also think it's the perfect way for everyone to be. In the course of self-creating our covers we begin to lose perspective. The lines of definition blur between God as the Creator and ourselves as God's creatures. We will soon claim to be our own creators. And we will boast about our creation: our *idealized self-image.*

Another part of our original gift will be denied. This will become our lifetime *avoidance.* Carl Jung referred to this as our "shadow." In Christian spirituality, this whole construct of the idealized self-image and the avoidance is considered to be a partial result of our fall from grace in original sin. It is helpful to remember that the word "sin" means a departure from what was originally intended. In the next chapter we will look at the avoidances. However, in this chapter we will describe the idealized self-image which has been developed by each Number. Since we began in the previous chapters with the Eight-Nine-One persons, we'll begin with the Two-Three-Four persons here, for the sake of variety. Let's start, though, with some self-observation.

SELF-OBSERVATION JOURNAL:
Read through the list of words given here. Choose ten to twelve words which are qualities that others would use to describe you.

thoughtful	unique	cooperative	invincible	right
productive	observant	happy ✓	easygoing	caring
✓different	dutiful	strong	good	admired
thorough	terrific	agreeable	attentive	elegant
loyal	prevailing	controlled	joyful	calm
studious	successful	tender	distinctive ✓	trusting
sturdy	accepting	conscientious	creative	curious ✓
delightful	energetic ✓	self-assertive	theorist	fun ✓
✓enthusiastic	disciplined	receptive	compassionate ✓	inspired
✓responsible	determined	efficient	researcher	versatile
supportive	goal-setter	principled ✓	spontaneous	private
speculative	sympathetic	individualist ✓	trustworthy	patient
confident	humorous ✓	accomplisher	insightful	ethical
exuberant	dependable	charming	needed	kind
positive	forceful	profound	changeable ✓	reliable
idealistic	peaceful	knowledgeable	expansive	settled
✓authentic	unusual	hard worker ✓	good worker ✓	giving ✓
powerful	generous	good image	original ✓	expert
helpful	attractive	sensitive ✓	perceptive	vigilant
lighthearted	confrontive	comfortable	committed	fair
appropriate	content	protective	planner	intuitive
✓interdependent	all together	intimate	honorable	warm
nurturing	accommodating	noble	achiever	special ✓
exquisite	forthright	reassuring	crusader	relaxed
tireless	progressive	orderly	wise	free

The next pages describe *the idealized self-images* of each of the Numbers. As you read the following descriptions, notice in which Number you find most of your chosen words.

THE TWO: I CARE ONLY ABOUT YOU AND YOUR NEEDS

The Twos in the self-creation of an idealized self-image choose the quality of **caring** as the best of all qualities. The Twos then will focus chiefly on being perfectly attentive to the needs of others. They will try to always ask about others' needs with sincere and loving interest. The question "How are you?" will be a serious question to which Twos truly hope to get an in-depth answer. They will not be able to feel good about themselves until the others they are attending to open up and share their needs. The Twos will offer sympathy and give assistance, showing concern and compassion for all those in their lives. If these offers are accepted, the Twos will feel needed and important to the other persons. This will reassure the Twos that their ideal of being a **perfectly caring person** is being attained. Others will recognize the Twos as generous and helpful persons. The Twos want to be close to others physically and emotionally. They have a warm and intimate way of approaching others. They do not share themselves intimately. This would go against the ideal. The focus of care and involvement must always be on others. At the risk of being intrusive, the Twos will move towards others with a nurturing caress of the hand or offer a warm and tender hug as they ask the other person about feelings. They try personally to touch the hearts of others, too, remembering others' hopes and dreams, as well as their birthdays. The Twos like to feel important in others' lives. This is their verification that others value them as perfectly caring people. And, this is what the Twos' idealized self-image is self-created to say: "I care only about you and your needs."

THE THREE: I AM PRODUCTIVE AND SUCCESSFUL

The Threes will self-create an idealized self-image on the basic of the quality of **success**. All the creative energy of the Threes will be poured into achieving one thing and then the next. They will seek to be efficient in setting goals and to be productive in their accomplishments. The Threes will be conscious of the image they are creating. Others will admire them as outstanding. This will give the Threes the positive response they seek for their creation of a **perfectly successful person.** They will be valued as very attractive people who seem to "have it all together." If for some reason their efforts are not admired, they will adapt their roles or redefine their public images. They will do whatever might lead to a greater promise of success. Then they will rechannel their energies toward more impressive progress. They are seeking to be a perfect example of success. The best progress and the sharpest image are both very important and go hand in hand. The Threes identify themselves with roles, whether they be entrepreneurs, professionals, politicians, academics, parents, media personalities or whatever. The Threes will evaluate their own personal worth by evaluating their successes in these roles. Their idealized self-image is developed to say: "I am productive and successful."

THE FOUR: I AM UNIQUE . . . DIFFERENT

The Fours' idealized self-image will be self-created around the quality of **uniqueness**. It will be distinctive, elegant, charming, unlike any other. The Four will use the whole person, body-mind-emotions, to communicate this ideal self in a most unusual way. Fours will dress imaginatively, use language differently and move their bodies in very conscious and purposeful ways. And, most importantly, their feelings will somehow be expressed in this special self-presentation. The mood which their feelings evoke is also quite important. They will value their self-image as ideal because it will be a wonderfully inspired and artistic expression of their very individual person. The normal, everyday, ordinary, natural presentation of personhood will not be enough for the Fours. To be a **perfectly unique person** they must, in a sense, breathe life into life before it can be considered truly authentic. The Four, seeking perfect originality, will not only be self-aware but also sensitive and intuitive regarding others' emotions. The Fours will demonstrate a desire to touch others emotionally. The personal and revealing sharing of themselves will be what the Fours feel is their most exquisite gift. If it is refused they may be deeply depressed. If their gift of self is received gratefully, the Fours will feel they have been recognized in their self-created idealized self-image which says: "I am unique . . . different."

THE FIVE: I AM KNOWLEDGEABLE

The Fives will self-create an idealized self-image around the quality of being **knowledgeable.** They will want to send forth the message to others that they know and understand everything. They will be very observant and thorough in their study of everything under the sun. They will thoroughly research, theorize and speculate about all the questions that provoke their curiosity. The Fives may spend a great deal of private time in these activities. They would prefer to discover knowledge by themselves so they don't have to show anyone that they are less than **perfectly knowledgeable persons**. They are quite perceptive and can be very insightful, often profound. However, it will be important for others to remain in the position of the one who seeks knowledge. This allows the Five to be the one who disseminates the knowledge, the expert. Only in that style of relationship can the Five be the one who is perfectly knowledgeable. Of course, the Five will always be collecting more and more information because one idea or fact leads to another. As with all Numbers, it is an ongoing challenge to create and maintain the idealized self-image that says: "I am knowledgeable."

THE SIX: I AM COOPERATIVE:
DUTIFUL, LOYAL AND RESPONSIBLE

The Sixes self-create an idealized self-image around the concept of **cooperation.** The Sixes seek to please other people by reacting positively to whatever their expectations may be. Sixes choose to trust that others know best how life should be lived. When other people make requests, the Sixes work very hard to do what's expected. And they are good workers, very reliable and trustworthy. They not only meet the request but worry about whether or not they have done it right, "the way it was supposed to be done." They also worry that they might get caught doing it wrong. In this context, right and wrong are not intended in a moral sense. Here they simply mean "according to the way it was expected to be done" by the one who made the request. This is why others value Sixes as dependable. Sixes display a kind of happiness to be of service if they know what is expected of them. Each opportunity to serve brings them closer to their idealized self-image. Sixes not only meet requests but vigilantly look for ways that they could be a **perfectly cooperative person,** someone who is pleasing to others. They like the interdependence of a group, all members honoring one anothers' requests and responsibilities. The Sixes may ask permission of others before doing something. This is usually done when Sixes suspect that they might disappoint or anger others. Seeking permission keeps the Sixes safe from possibly offending the powers-that-be. And, for the Sixes, the powers-that-be could be anyone they hope to please and not disappoint. The Sixes identify some others as authorities. They then become committed to pleasing these authorities. The Sixes' idealized self-image is self-created to say: "I am cooperative: dutiful, loyal and responsible."

THE SEVEN: I AM HAPPY AND LIFE IS TERRIFIC

The Sevens self-create an idealized self-image, making the quality of **happiness** central. The Sevens will seek to guarantee that every moment of life will be a happy experience. All of the past will have a joyfulness to it, and the negative factors will be explained away. The future has unlimited potential and the promise of abundant enjoyment. The present can be filled with delight if the Seven can make it so. Being in the Center compelled by fear, the Sevens put forth tremendous effort to keep their idealized self-image of happiness in place. They use their enthusiasm, exuberance, spontaneity and versatility to keep the general mood ever-changing. They keep cheering themselves on with sayings like the following: "Keep it light and humorous and fun. Don't let it slip into sadness or depression. Keep changing the experiences. Don't let things stagnate. We could get stuck in boredom. Keep the options open and the energy flowing freely. Don't lock into commitment. Appreciate every little thing. Don't miss one sensation." Sevens use their hyperactive minds to keep planning more and more diversions and escapes from the dread of gloom and deprivation. They must appear as **perfectly happy persons** and their lives must seem perfectly delightful. All their lively activity and apparent lightheartedness keeps their idealized self-image in place. Their self-created image is saying: "I am happy and life is terrific."

THE EIGHT: I AM INVINCIBLE

The Eights self-create an idealized self-image based on the quality of being **invincible**. The Eights will use all their strength to assure that no one and no thing will ever conquer their spirits. They will insist on their strong wills prevailing. They will glow with pride over their sturdiness, assertiveness and determination. Eights use their confidence to take charge and control all situations. Coming from the Gut-Instinct Center, the Eights will use their bodies to communicate that they are perfectly invincible persons. They make grand, expansive gestures and dominate with a forceful physical presence. They are very self-assertive, making themselves physically at home wherever they happen to be. They take a bold approach to all situations. They will act in powerfully protective ways on behalf of those they sense as most vulnerable in this world. They will be forthright in their advocacy for others. The Eights distrust that anyone other than themselves is strong enough to keep life and limb together for them. They must do this themselves. Sometimes unavoidable situations occur where the Eights have to put themselves in others' hands. In these cases, they will test the one in charge, sometimes through a confrontation, to verify that this leader will be strong enough to care for them. Their idealized self-image says it all: "I am invincible."

THE NINE: I AM EASYGOING AND AGREEABLE

The Nines self-create their idealized self-image from the quality of being **agreeable**. According to the Nines, the best choice to make in life is to agree with the others. Don't rock the boat. Go along to get along. The Nines are very accepting and supportive of others' preferences and plans. They are open and receptive to others while being self-effacing toward themselves. This gives others the impression that the Nines are patient and peaceful in their interactions. Actually, at some level beneath the surface, the Nines are struggling very hard to keep this ideal self-image in place. This is the **perfectly agreeable person**. Nine. Externally, they seem so content and comfortable with their positions (or non-positions) in various matters. If they are challenged for being too accommodating, they will reassure the other that "it really makes no difference; it doesn't matter." The Nine who is focused on this ideal self will seem very calm and relaxed. In actuality, this lack of activity is probably exhaustion. It takes a lot of energy to produce this settled manner. The Nines work hard to be sure their idealized self-image says: "I am easygoing and agreeable."

THE ONE: I AM RIGHT AND GOOD AND IN CONTROL OF MYSELF

The Ones self-create their idealized self-image from the quality of being **good.** The only choice Ones feel they have is to be good and to do good always. One false step and it's all out of control. Their "parent tapes" are very clear and very critical. They must always be conscientious in their work and emotionally disciplined. They maintain very high principles of behavior and demand strict compliance from themselves. They seem to be naturally ethical and idealistic. Among their ideals is the strong belief that they must be in control of themselves at all times and in all things. They must be consistent in their work, proper in their social dealings and act appropriately in all situations. The Ones' idealized self-image is not only about their being good and upright, but also about their doing good and noble deeds. The One must be a **perfectly good person** in all ways.

Because of this, Ones work relentlessly and tirelessly to bring more goodness into the world. The Ones are crusaders and reformers. They will work for any cause that promises to bring fair treatment to all. No matter how hard working the Ones are, they will still continue to criticize themselves for not being better, doing more for more people, and so forth. The idealized self-image which the Ones have self-created says: "I am right and good and in control of myself."

ALL DIFFERENT, YET THE SAME

These are the covers, the idealized self-images we have all developed for protection. They look somewhat like the real thing, the God-gift, but they are just good imitations. We can tell the difference by the desperation each Number shows in creating and maintaining these perfect covers. The God-gift, as we will see later, flows freely, comes naturally. However, the idealized self-image is maintained at great price to each person. No matter how we feel or what we think or what events occur, we must always respond in this same ideal way. Therefore, we often must repress our feelings, deny our thoughts and ignore the reality of events. This is frequently the only way we can keep our idealized self-images in place. And, we will continue to force ourselves into this unreal ideal as long as we believe we need to protect ourselves from something dreadful. This "something dreadful" is the other part of the gift which we have denied. We will discuss this in the next chapter on Avoidances.

SELF-OBSERVATION JOURNAL:

Now that you have read about the nine *idealized self-images*, which one(s) seemed most like you?

Each of the nine descriptions include words from the list you looked at in the beginning of this chapter. Compare the descriptions which seem most like you with your list of ten to twelve chosen words.

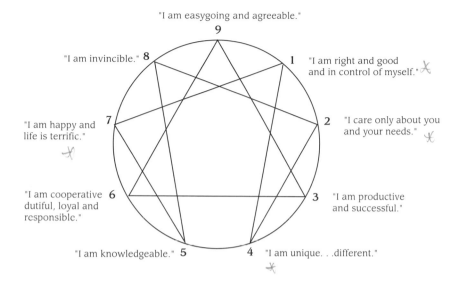

Figure Five

If your self-observation is on target, you may well find that the majority of your chosen words are all in one of the descriptions. If you cannot find a correlation between your list of chosen words and the one description which seems most like you, remember this is a journey. Keep traveling.

CHAPTER EIGHT

Our Avoidances and Defense Mechanisms

YOU ARE NOT ACCEPTABLE AS YOU ARE

As suggested in the previous chapter, there is another part of our original giftedness that we deny. As was mentioned earlier, there was a time when we thought we heard others saying: "You are not acceptable as you are." And one thing we did to prevent this from recurring was to create our cover, the *idealized self-image*. This was our insurance against the possibility of personal attacks in the future. This cover we created actually concealed from others another part of ourselves we considered bad, defective or lacking in some way. As we hid this part from others, it gradually became disowned by us. Eventually, we denied it even existed. In Enneagram terms, this denied part of us is called our *avoidance*. So we see that the cover works in two directions. It presents an ideal self to the world, and it seals off from view what we ourselves have decided is the unacceptable part of our being. The recognition of our avoidance will be the key to future growth and development.

We must rediscover what we are working so hard to avoid recognizing and accepting about ourselves. Unless we can reclaim our avoidance as part of us, we cannot be whole. We will not be able to retrieve our full giftedness.

However, the avoidance is not only covered from outside view by the idealized self-image. It is also guarded from our own inner recognition by our *defense mechanisms.* Since these defenses prevent us from gaining personal awareness of the avoidance, it's hard for us to rediscover it. As human beings we all use several defense mechanisms. It is possible, though, to identify the particular defense that we each use most regularly. This could be considered our most preferred defense or our defense of choice.

Claudio Naranjo, a well known psychiatrist who has been a pioneer in the study and teaching of the Enneagram, has theorized that each Enneagram Number generally employs one defense more exclusively and more often than the others. He has applied specific defense mechanisms to each of the nine Enneagram Numbers. So although we may not be able easily to identify our avoidance, it is more likely that we will be able to identify our defense of choice. Once we have identified the defense, it will lead us to a certain Enneagram number and that particular avoidance. Again, for the sake of variety, the descriptions of avoidances and defense mechanisms will begin with the Five-Six-Seven persons. But before describing the avoidances and defense mechanisms, let's do some journaling.

SELF-OBSERVATION JOURNAL:

SITUATION: You are unexpectedly and suddenly fired from your job. The Personnel Manager reads your "dismissal slip" to you. "You are no longer needed in our employ. Your training and abilities are not of value to us at this time. Your reliability, commitment and durability are lass than we had expected. You are an unacceptable employee for our firm."

IN WHICH OF THE FOLLOWING WAYS WOULD YOU MOST LIKELY RESPOND TO THE PERSONNEL MANAGER?

- (With an edge of anger in your voice and negative emotions bubbling internally:)

   "Thank you very much. You've done a good job of explaining all this."

- "It must be very hard for you to give this kind of news to people."

- "You must be mistaken. Your company really needs me and my talents to get back up on top of the competition."

- "I could feel this loss coming. Isn't it ironic that life is a series of losses."

- "It's very interesting to see how you go about your job of letting people go."

- "It's your fault. You should have told me what you wanted."

- "This is great. It frees me up to look into a lot of other options that I would really enjoy."

- "Your fancy words just cover up your inability to make use of my talents."

- "Don't worry. It's no big deal. I've got a lot to keep me busy with at home."

WHICH RESPONSE WOULD BE YOURS IN THIS SITUATION?

These are all examples of various defense mechanisms we use to protect ourselves from being hurt by that dreaded message: "You are unacceptable as you are." As you read the following pages, you will see descriptions of the most basic defenses used by each of the Nine Numbers. The examples on this page will fit those descriptions, though these are in order from Numbers One to Nine.

THE FIVE: AVOIDANCE AND DEFENSE

The Five seeks to avoid **not knowing**. In the more immediate sense, this involves not knowing what's happening in the moment. It can be quite embarrassing for a Five not to know how to act in various situations. At a much deeper level, not knowing for a Five relates to all that happens in life. The Fives need to know about and understand beforehand all that will be involved in every life event and every encounter with others. Not knowing beforehand leaves the Five open to the unpredictability of surprise or spontaneous encounters. These situations are seen as potentially threatening to a Five because the outcome is not predictable. The Fives feel the need to regulate both internal and external influences. By insisting on knowing, they seek to regulate both their internal feelings as well as the external control which may come from others. The Fives fear being unexpectedly overwhelmed by life. This fear keeps them in a constant search for knowledge and meaning, the knowledge of everyday events and the meaning of life itself. At all costs, the Fives will use their defense of choice to avoid not knowing.

The Fives most preferred defenses are **isolation and compartmentalization.** When the threat of being overwhelmed by unpredictability or meaninglessness emerges, it activates fear in the Five. This will trigger the defense to go into operation. The Fives will separate their ideas and their actions from their feelings. They will, in a sense, put each in a separate compartment. When feelings are separated out, this allows the Five to interact with life in an abstract and objective way. The Five can now analyze from a safe distance what is happening in life. In this defensive process, certain parts of the Five's person become isolated from the others. And eventually the Five becomes isolated from experiencing life. When the various parts of ourselves are isolated, life experiences lose their emotional charge. Then the threat subsides, and the Fives can go on functioning in a safe and predictable way. In this mode the Fives think they know what's happening to them and therefore can stay in control of the events of life. Of course, if too much energy is siphoned off by this process, the Fives will begin to view life as meaningless again. So, they will have to regulate the gates on the various compartments. This will allow some of the parts to come together now and then, but not too often and not too much. These processes of isolation and compartmentalization will continue until the Five chooses to recognize the avoidance of not knowing.

THE SIX: AVOIDANCE AND DEFENSE

The Sixes avoid **uncertainty**. On an everyday basis, the Sixes want to be certain about the schedule, the agenda, the map, and all the expectations others have for them. On a lifetime basis, the Sixes want to be certain they can trust that God is in heaven and that we are family. When the Six discovers that life or individual people are not what the Six has believed them to be, this can provoke a great amount of fear. If the fear is disturbing enough, it will catapult the Six into high anxiety. To relieve this anxiety, the Six will employ the defense of choice to avoid uncertainty.

The Sixes' chosen defense is **projection.** This means to take what the Six is feeling internally and project it outwards into another. This externalizes the feeling of fear as if it belongs to another person. Consequently, the Six can shift the responsibility or blame onto the other person for creating the climate of uncertainty. For example, the Six might say: "It's your job to tell people exactly what to do. You're not doing a very good job or else we wouldn't have so many different approaches. How are we supposed to choose?" The Six will continually use **projection** as a defense whenever fear arises. Someday, perhaps the growth choice will be made to recognize the avoidance of **uncertainty.**

THE SEVEN: AVOIDANCE AND DEFENSE

The Sevens avoid **sadness**. In its broadest definition, sadness is the feeling of being deprived of joy. Deprivation in all its forms is what reduces the Sevens to a state of sadness. The Sevens seek emotional happiness as well as physical enjoyment. They want to be happy in the present, recall wonderful times of the past and look forward in an upbeat manner to the future. The Sevens want to be reassured that life will always be a delightful experience. Or better yet, they hope for life to be a never-ending series of only delightful experiences. So when real life intrudes with its inevitable negative overtones, it threatens to trap them in sadness. In fear of deprivation, the Sevens then will quickly move to shield themselves from these negative aspects of reality.

For the Seven, the most common defense is **intellectual sublimation.** All of us rationalize at times when we consciously give excuses for what others judge to be our unacceptable behavior. However, intellectual sublimation is an unconscious version of this process. When the Sevens make light of tragedy, they are not just trying to make the accompanying bad feelings go away. They are also actively struggling to prevent the deprivation of joy. They are actually using their creative mental ability to reframe the event itself. For example, if they were to lose in a competition they would probably say right away, "There must be some good reason why this is happening to me." Through the use of their chosen defense, they will recreate the event in their minds so that it now has a positive purpose. Sevens will also use this defense to reconnect unacceptable emotions or urges to acceptable action. For cxample, if they have aggressive urges they might channel them into a boxing career. If they love food to the point of overeating they might become master chefs. No matter how **intellectual sublimation** is used for defense, the Sevens will succeed in their avoidance of **sadness.**

THE EIGHT: AVOIDANCE AND DEFENSE

The Eights avoid **vulnerability.** Any situation which activates a feeling of weakness will be avoided by Eights. They will do whatever they need to do to be sure they are physically safe and strong. And, they will also secure a safe emotional atmosphere for themselves. The Eights are very clear about what they want and don't want to happen to them or in their surroundings. As long as the Eights choose to avoid weakness, they will not allow their soft and tender feelings to be emotionally aroused. As soon as the threat of this looms on the horizon of their lives, they will move to defend against it.

The Eights choose the defense of **denial.** This is a strong and direct defense. It is very uncomplicated. The Eights simply state or will that something isn't so. "My eyes might be watering but I'm not crying. I never cry." Whatever is unacceptable, by willing it out of existence, just isn't so for the Eight. To the listener the Eights may seem uncaring or unfeeling. However, this defense has not been tailored for the listener. It is employed by the Eight for the protection of the Eight. Contrary to what seems to be the case, Eights are filled with warm, soft feelings. Yet denial will keep these feelings from showing because the Eights are impelled to avoid **vulnerability.**

THE NINE: AVOIDANCE AND DEFENSE

The Nines avoid **discord.** Anything that might be upsetting, conflictual or possibly cause chaos is avoided by the Nines. One of the most common examples is seen in Nines' aversion to decision making. They have an ability to outlast any other person in a discussion pointed towards a decision. Out of exasperation others will usually end up making the decision. For Nines to decide involves taking a stand or setting a course. This leaves them open to the disagreement of others. This could result in discord. It's just better to go with the flow. There is also an inner turmoil with which the Nines must contend. When the events of life threaten to disturb the inner calm of the Nines, they will defend themselves against this upsetting intrusion.

The Nines choose the defense of **narcotization.** This term suggests being artificially put to sleep or put into a different mental state. This other mental state is one which deadens us to reality so we can no longer feel it. Some Nines actually do overuse chemicals, including food, to shut out reality. However, chemicals and food are not even necessary for a Nine who effectively uses mental distraction to narcotize against reality. For example, as soon as there is a hint of something which could upset their inner calm, the Nines will allow their attention to wander. If a certain issue seems threatening, they will free-associate from that one to whatever it may remind them of in another realm of thought. For example, if the sudden mention of an overdue *bill* begins to upset them, they might just recall a friend named *Bill* they saw yesterday, and so on. By distracting themselves, they move their mental energy away from the conflict and toward a neutral issue. What the Nines are seeking to do is to put themselves into a mental state other than the one that is full of discord. With their defense of **narcotization** the Nines can avoid **discord** and return to inner calm.

THE ONE: AVOIDANCE AND DEFENSE

The Ones' avoidance is **incompletion and limitation.** Anything that is not complete, finished and perfect is to be avoided. The strongest examples of this are those parts of the Ones which they themselves judge as incomplete or limited. Any behavior that is less than the ideal is imperfect. Any emotion that is negative is unacceptable. Any thought considered improper is labeled bad. Many of the naturally occurring thoughts, feelings and behaviors of the Ones are considered by them to be unacceptable according to the high standards of perfection they hold as ultimate. When these unacceptable yet naturally occurring reactions erupt, the Ones use their defense mechanism.

The Ones' most common defense is **reaction formation.** By way of definition, this means to act in a way opposite to how one actually feels. For example, for the Ones the feelings of jealousy or anger are considered to be bad. According to the Ones, these feelings are not what a perfect and complete human being should feel. Perfect people should be loving, generous and kind. This is what the Ones learned in their early years as they were being formed into good girls and good boys. So what do they do now in adulthood when something happens which stirs anger or jealousy in them? They cannot tolerate experiencing much less expressing these emotions. Instead, they express the reactions learned in formation. Love everyone and rejoice for their good fortune. Therefore, the internally angry One will externally express only happy feelings for the other person. This defensive use of reaction formation will help the Ones avoid being imperfect: incomplete or limited as human beings.

THE TWO: AVOIDANCE AND DEFENSE

The Twos' avoidance is **neediness, their own neediness.** Sometimes it seems as if the Twos are saying they simply are not like the rest of us. They just do not have any needs. At other times, Twos may sound more like they're saying that they are not worthy enough to have needs or to request help. Naturally, the Twos have needs as all humans do. However, their own neediness must be avoided at all costs to preserve the idealized self-image of "the person who cares only for others' needs." So any needs or desires which threaten to emerge are met with the Twos' defense mechanism.

The Twos' most reliable defense is **repression**. In this case, the Twos don't deny their needs or turn them into something else as other Numbers do with their avoidances. Rather, the Twos block their needs from consciousness. The result is that they no longer consciously recognize their own needs. However, the feelings which accompany this process do make themselves known. The Twos may express these feelings indirectly in the emotion they attach to their words. They may state very absolutely that they have no needs. But the listener will hear hurt or anger in their tones. At times it is as if they "protest too much." This defense of **repression** will give the Twos the false assurance that they are avoiding **their own neediness.**

THE THREE: AVOIDANCE AND DEFENSE

The Threes' avoidance is **nothingness.** Any suggestion that the Threes are nothing or what they do amounts to nothing would be considered failure to them. This must be avoided at all costs to maintain the idealized self-image of a productive and successful person. For any of us to know we are successful, we need to have affirmation of this from others, from the community. The Threes choose this community of others in many different forms. It may be one's parents, a special person, one's own family, a group of close friends, various segments of the larger society, and so forth. The Threes will avoid whatever their chosen group indicates is unsuccessful behavior. When life for Threes turns out in unexpected ways and failure looms, the Threes will move to defend against this threat.

The Threes' choice of defense is identification. Whatever is successful will be claimed or owned. Whatever is not successful will be disowned. The Threes will personally identify with their successes, and only the successes. For example, if they design a new car, they may name if after themselves or at least let everyone know that they designed it. If they created a lemon they may lay the claim at someone else's feet. Or they will somehow sell the idea that they actually intended to create a lemon all along, perhaps for research purposes. With the use of this defense of identification, the Threes will successfully avoid nothingness and keep their idealized self-image intact: I am productive and successful.

THE FOUR: AVOIDANCE AND DEFENSE

The Fours' avoidance is **commonness or ordinariness.** What all the other Numbers think of as regular reality seems common to the Fours. Others might be content, even grateful, to experience a simple, trouble-free day. To Fours this would be a gray, colorless day. Simply to feel fine or O.K., content or nice, would seem flat and dull, like gray cardboard, to the Fours. To be methodical and logical, attending to details, would be boring and uncreative for the Fours. All of life that is perceived in these ways by the Fours must be avoided. Therefore, there is a moment-to-moment defensive operation in action.

The Fours' defense is **artistic sublimation.** This is similar to the Sevens' mental reframing of painful reality into positive experiences. The issue for Fours, however, is not to avoid sadness but to avoid commonness. So the Fours will transform gray, colorless days, flat emotions and boring activity into something much more meaningful. The Fours' re-creation process will involve their emotions and creativity. For example, the Fours might draw out all the shades and hues of gray and create a whole kaleidoscope of gray tones. They might then transform this vision into a poem or a piece of music. Whatever course this process of **artistic sublimation** may take, the Fours are willing and able to go to the highest and lowest levels of the emotional scale. Anything to avoid **commonness and ordinariness:** the predictable, certain and safe middle points of life.

These are the ways we protect ourselves from the attacks we fear. If we can defend against our avoidances surfacing, we can maintain our idealized self-images.

SELF-OBSERVATION JOURNAL:

In comparing yourself to the nine **avoidances** just described, with which one do you most identify? Write about certain examples in your life which demonstrate how you avoid whatever it is you do avoid.

Figure Six

Of all **defense mechanisms** described, which one seemed most familiar to you? Describe some of the ways you use this defense.

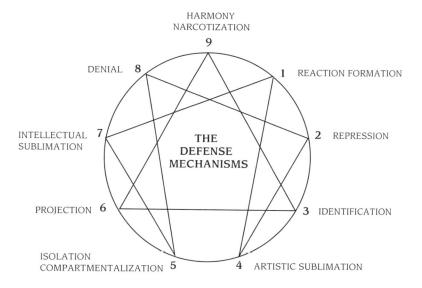

Figure Seven

CHAPTER NINE

From Compulsion to Giftedness

OUR PASSIONS AND VIRTUES

As was explained in the last chapter, we each strive to avoid a specific part of ourselves. We avoid this part because we find it somehow unacceptable. We also fear that if this part were known it would sabotage the presentation we try to make of an idealized self. The intensity of these two energies, to avoid a part of ourselves and to present ourselves ideally, will look different from one person to another. They will also differ in intensity from one period of our lives to another, from our peaceful days to more stressful times. The more stressful we are, the more our inner negative passion will ignite these energies. In our more peaceful times, we tend to be more open to growth. The result of such growth will be recognized by a decrease in our negative *passion* and an increase in the *virtue* of our *giftedness*.

Each of the nine Enneagram Numbers has a particular passion. When this passion flows, it is like molten lava consuming all life in its path, leaving behind only debris and destruction. The stronger the flow of passion the more we feel driven to push away from our avoidances and toward our idealized self-images. In today's terminology we refer to this as "compulsion." However, when this lava flow of our passions is halted and the sea breezes of spiritual openness abound, new forms of life emerge from the blackened terrain of our lives. The new forms of life which emerge are the Nine virtues of our various giftedness. As we travel along on our lifegrowth journeys, our hope is to move from *compulsion* to *giftedness*. However, before we know where the journey will take us, we have to see where we are. We need to recognize our compulsion in order to open to our giftedness.

Before reading the nine descriptions of compulsion and giftedness that follow here, let's do some journaling.

SELF-OBSERVATION JOURNAL:

(1) Observe yourself, or recall yourself, at times of high intensity, In what areas of your life do you feel driven? What do you feel compelled to do? Journal about yourself and these compelling drives. After journaling, consider the nine attitudes which follow.

(2) Which of these nine attitudes describes you best when your negative passion about life is the strongest?

ONE: It's very irritating to me when things or people are not the way they should be. I feel driven to fix them.

TWO: I love to find ways to meet the needs of others. I feel driven to help people.

THREE: I am invigorated and energized by goals and projects. I feel driven to keep moving from one accomplishment to the next.

FOUR: I feel intensely about all of life. I feel compelled to make every moment special.

FIVE: It's very scary for me to interact spontaneously with others in life. I feel compelled to figure things out before becoming involved.

SIX: I'm never sure I'm safe from all that could go wrong. I feel compelled to know what I'm supposed to do, think and say.

SEVEN: The thought of being deprived of fun or trapped in any way is terrifying. I feel driven to keep my spirit light and free.

EIGHT: It makes me angry to experience weakness in others. I am compelled to bring my power to bear on the situation.

NINE: It is upsetting for me to be bothered by anything or anyone. I feel compelled to keep things calm and peaceful.

Now return to the reading to learn about the *compulsions* and *giftedness* of each Enneagram Number.

THE ONES

The word which most precisely involves the Ones' energy is **standards.** According to the way the Ones operate, life has come to us imprinted with standards. Like the eagle stalking its prey, the One must keep a sharp eye out for all that does not measure up to the inherent standards which govern all of life.

In **compulsion** the Ones become the controller of the standards. Every bit of life begins and ends with adherence to the standards. These standards are not like rules that have been discussed, agreed upon and written down by some for all. Rather, it's as if the instincts of the Ones are engraved with the original standards. Ones instinctively sense how people, life and the world should be. In the compulsive state, the Ones cannot help but recognize any and all things which do not meet these standards of perfection. They cannot resist this drive within them which seeks to shape things up, to fix or at least to improve everything and everyone. It must be done. When this drive is strongest those who are on the receiving end will feel instructed, criticized, judged or even scolded and reprimanded. The Ones themselves profess to be well meaning and only telling others what is "for their own good." There is a sense of urgency in the Ones. It seems that they have reasoned that if we don't shape up quickly we will be caught and then "it's" all over. This, of course, is how the Ones feel about themselves. All this driving, controlling energy is employed for one reason. The Ones want to avoid being judged as bad or wrong, a mistake-maker, limited or imperfect in any way. And, of course, the rest of us mistake-makers are part of the problem even more so because we don't seem to care. Many people who know Ones refer to them as perfectionists. Ones themselves say, "Oh no, not me. You would never say that if you saw what my house or office looks like." For the Ones, the result of being judged bad will be a condemnation and separation. They are so conscientious that they want to warn us that this too could happen to us. However, the warnings only seem to make people angry, make people want to get away from the Ones' influence. So the Ones suffer the dreaded separation even as they strive to prevent it from happening. When faced with their compulsion, sometimes the Ones can admit to it and even laugh about it. At other times they feel too threatened by what they construe to be criticism rather than seeing it as a lifeline. Ones will hear the message only if they can believe the messenger loves them unconditionally.

In their most **gifted** state, the Ones have a much broader view of standards and perfection. They take the standards as guidelines or ideals to work toward. They embrace the idea that total perfection is that which will occur for all of us the day *after* we die. In the meantime, here in the land of the living, there can be some sense of perfection in every moment, every day. Each day is a part of a great long journey. And each moment, each step on the journey has a perfection of its own. Each square of a sidewalk seems to be nothing but a block of cement. Yet each square is essentially important in itself as a part of the whole. All the squares taken together will eventually complete the whole sidewalk. In their giftedness Ones know in theory that it is wrong to expect too much. The toddler who is taking her first unstable steps can't be expected to be walking by day's end or skipping rope by week's end. All of life is a process involving steps. In education there is a formula by which a curriculum is developed. First year: introduce a new concept (adding and subtracting single digits); second year: practice the concept (adding and subtracting double and triple digits); third year: master the concept (multiply and divide). The great gift that the Ones have to offer is simply to hold out the beacon for themselves and for all of us to sail toward as we navigate on our journey through life. Instead of being furious that everything is in such a mess, the gifted One, as the Serenity Prayer suggests, will have the serenity to accept the things that cannot be changed, the courage to change the things that can be changed, and (most importantly) the wisdom to know the difference. This will be the guiding light on the lifegrowth journey of Ones from the passion of anger to the virtue of serenity.

THE TWOS

The word around which the Twos focus all their energies is **need.** It's as if this is the main thing, sometimes the only thing, the Twos see or hear or feel. They pick up on needs by listening and intuiting through the language of feelings.

In their **compulsive** state, the Twos will be constantly involved with other people's needs. They will feel the needs, name them for others and meet those needs. Their whole focus will be on people and on taking care of them. They will give advice, whether it's requested or not. They will flatter and comfort others. They will compliment people on anything and everything. For example, if you've just said "hello" on the phone, a Two may compliment you on your voice. Their tenderness is often expressed by physically touching others. In compulsion, their emotional expressiveness may even become effusive. For them it is a vital need to connect with people and develop caring, loving relationships. For the most part these will be one-way streets. Oftentimes, unknown to themselves, the Twos may be experiencing a feeling of sadness, loneliness or hurt. Instead of recognizing their own need for comfort, they will project this feeling onto another who seems to have a similar need, "Oh, you look so sad." In compulsion, much of the Twos' involvement with others represents an attempt to avoid their own neediness. The more they cater to others' needs the farther away they get from receiving care for themselves. When they encounter a situation in which they feel unappreciated, they often become angry toward those with whom they had hoped to share love. This progression will eventually lead the Twos to try to dominate and possess others or, if that is not possible, produce guilt feelings in them. Their opportunities to awaken will come through the loving care of others' confrontation, or perhaps through their own burnout.

In the most **gifted** state, the Twos will feel that they, too, have needs, especially a need to be loved and cared for. They also will be able to love and care for themselves first before they reach out to others. It will be apparent to them that the only healthy way to help others is by keeping themselves on balance. This balancing of personal needs with the needs of others is well illustrated by the airline pilot who tells passengers with children to put on their own oxygen masks first before assisting their children. The Twos must learn to care for themselves first and not seek care and appreciation as a reward for helping others. In their giftedness the Twos will know when and to whom they should offer help. They also will ask others if they need and want help rather than intrusively insist on helping. They will help others most by modeling good self-caretaking. Being honest and open about their own frailties and needs will probably be the greatest gift they will give to others. This self-revelation will remind us all of our frail humanity. It will be a message that reminds us of our universal need for a Higher Power in our lives. This truth is well capsulized in Henri Nouwen's book *The Wounded Healer* when he says that "the wounded healer is a hospitable host." The growing Twos will eventually let go of their feeling of being indispensable and embrace their wounded humanness. This is the evolution which occurs for the Twos on the lifegrowth journey from the **passion of pride** to the **virtue of humility.**

THE THREES

The word which draws all the Threes' energy to the forefront is **goals.** The Threes are focused on setting goals, meeting goals, evaluating goals, and most importantly, in being evaluated by others according to the goals accomplished. They are constantly aware of how others interact with them and evaluate their accomplishments. The Threes acquire their identity through their connection to the community. In their **compulsion** the Threes are always intent on making and selling a product. This product may be an idea, a thing or even themselves. They set goals, lay out objectives and produce. It's as simple as 1-2-3. Then they listen for the response of the audience. Depending on what they hear in this response, they may make some minor adjustments or possibly even significant changes. All this adaptation is done without any apparent loss of self-esteem. Then they present their product again and try to sell it. The selling is also a 1-2-3 operation. A Three once said to me, "Selling is easy. It goes like this: Introduce yourself. Introduce your product. Sell yourself. Sell your product." Then without missing a step the Threes proceed to the next goal, with one eye on the audience. And the "audience" is anyone they have decided possesses the stature they admire. This audience will be the person or persons who can confer the applause they seek. In compulsion, the Threes are seeking to run from what they feel is their worthlessness, their nothingness. In the push to produce something outside themselves to sell, they unwittingly endorse their own suspicion that there is nothing inside of any worth. The Threes do not usually wake up from this compulsive state unless they suffer a devastating failure to reach their goal, or the audience leaves. Occasionally the Threes suffer a physical sidelining, such as a broken leg. This may stop the motion long enough for them to become introspective enough to rouse them from their compulsive state. Somehow, they have to hit the bottom. Then they either sink into depression or face themselves honestly.

In their most **gifted** state, the Threes direct all their energies toward the goal of developing themselves as full persons. They don't see themselves as the producers and salespersons of a product. Rather, they see that who they become as persons, from the inside out, is the real goal of life. The gifted "product" will result from the development of an inner life where they are aware of their own feelings and consciously connected to their own motivations. The growing Threes make the greatest use of their giftedness to produce something when they encourage others to make the most of themselves and their talents. The poet Charles Peguy wrote: "If you try to go to God alone God will surely ask you an embarrassing question: 'Where are your brothers and sisters?' " These lines seem written for the Threes. As a Chicago sports fan, let me offer an example. Often when Michael Jordan played as a one-man team, the Chicago Bulls lost. However, when he became the playmaker and got all his teammates to perform at their highest levels, the Bulls seemed to win. In retirement from basketball, Michael Jordan is building family recreation centers. He says, "Among our many social problems we have trouble giving our young people wholesome recreation. I feel that golf can be one more wholesome activity made available to young people. Golf teaches discipline, patience and determination. I've grown to love it and benefit from it as a person. I know that others can do the same and I just want to make it possible for more people to be introduced to the sport." This is the greatest use of the Threes' giftedness, to bring everyone along with them. When they do this, the Threes are admitting the basic truth: "I am nothing. I truly am nothing without other people." As this phase of the Threes' lifegrowth journey is reached, there is no more of the **passion of deceit,** only the **virtue of honesty**.

THE FOURS

The word which symbolizes all the energy of the Fours is **different.** The Fours feel that they are different from everyone else. And they feel intensely that all persons are different, one from another. They feel that they are themselves unique.

In **compulsion** this sense of differentness will manifest itself in various ways. On the one hand, the Fours try not to be different, to stand out in any way, for fear of rejection. However, they are so conscious of this that they try too hard to be accepted and end up being different. On the other hand, when they are treated as everyone else they seem to take offense at this. It's as if they are uncomfortable with themselves no matter how the situation presents itself. They view others as being accepted. They see themselves on the outside, with their noses pressed against the glass, looking in on life and longing to be accepted as others seem to be. This may sound strange to you if you are not a Four. However, it's also very bewildering for the Fours. They take it very seriously and very personally. They are the most emotionally sensitive of all the Numbers, and their emotions can gain ascendency over their whole persons. When their emotions take over, they can produce a state of anarchy, rendering the Fours unable to function. At this point, all they can say to others is something like, "I'm not in the mood." This is a clue that the emotions are in charge. The Fours will verbally agree that this is so, but this will only intensify their slide into self-absorption. They play a cat and mouse game with the feeling of being different. Their goal is to avoid commonness. But once they are different, this becomes the problem. Their anxiety and depression about being rejected for their commonness has driven them to risk rejection for their differentness. "Oh what a tangled web we weave when first we try to deceive." In their darkest hours, it is most important that they confide in those closest to them. It is only when they allow the daylight of objectivity into their emotional world that they will be able to awaken. This was expressed beautifully in a few short lines from a piece entitled *Ramblings of a Four* written by Lynne Brenan:

4 is like a moth flickering around a summer light
flitting to an fro'
attracted to the light but afraid of singeing its wings
if it gets too close
all the while fearful of losing its fragile
intricately beautiful wings
not knowing once it enters that light
it will cease to flitter and begin to soar!

In their most **gifted** state, the Fours will embrace their commonness as that which gives their life the texture of reality. It is their communality which connects them to all others. And the connection allows them to offer their gift of sensitivity to each individual and unique person. The Fours are able to interact with each person in a different way. This gives others a special sense of being loved for themselves. When the Fours reach out in this way, they also recover a feeling of increased self-esteem. They have a special gift to offer which has been appreciated by others. They are reaffirmed in their belief that there must be something attractive and non-rejectable about them. Each new positive feeling draws the Fours farther out of from their self-absorption. These positive feelings will activate more of the same emergence, and the Fours will recognize they have a special and very valuable contribution to make. They will no longer anguish over the fascination of differentness. Their feelings will not lock them into a state of inactive longing. They will recognize themselves as equal to all others joined in oneness. While they remain in touch with their feelings, they will balance this subjectivity with objectivity. This represents the Fours' lifegrowth journey from the **passion of envy** to the **virtue of equanimity.**

THE FIVES

The word which most clearly distills the Fives' energy is **observe.** The Fives are "all eyes." Life comes into them from this, their most prominent sense. With their eyes and their minds they try to observe and understand the mysteries of the world and everything in it. They work at understanding how it all fits together, how everything is interrelated. Then they ask a further question: What is the meaning of the whole?

In **compulsion** the Fives will avidly and persistently seek to observe more, learn more, understand more by fitting more and more pieces together. Their minds can become like spinning tops. They will usually focus on one or only a few topics at a time. They work in a tight circle moving inward to develop deeper and deeper levels of refinement for greater understanding. It's as if the Fives are looking for one perfect word or one single formula to express a whole field of knowledge. When they speak, you will hear their heads talking as they outline and summarize the topic of discussion. Or you might not hear them saying anything at all until the end of an encounter or meeting. Then they will offer a brief but brilliant summary line from their ivory tower. In order to accomplish all this objective observation, the Fives think that they have to remove themselves emotionally and sometimes physically from the world. When they withdraw into themselves, they are actually losing important ways to observe and collect information. Gradually their observations and conclusions about the world become more and more sterile and distorted. To maintain this stance, they will eventually move into a kind of eccentric life and perhaps even become reclusive. Their world will eventually have a population of one. In compulsion, they have sought desperately to understand the world so they could know how to fit into it. This compulsive process, however, has now resulted in removing them from the world. It takes the rawest kind of courage for a reclusive Five to reenter the world. Usually they need the gentle and repeated invitations of patient friends. Or perhaps they will wake up and reenter life if they somehow admit to themselves how desperately empty and alone they actually are.

In their most **gifted** state, the Fives will know and accept that they cannot know all that will make them feel able to fit safely into the world. They simply feel the need to get in there and relate, to enter the world. You cannot learn to swim without going into the water. Involvement in life will allay their fear of not knowing, which only intensifies their desire for isolation and private thinking time. Socrates said many centuries ago: "I only know that I know nothing." To try to know all about life without entering it is to miss out on knowing the most important things about life. Many other people feel themselves to be on the outside of life at various times and in various ways. It is to these people especially that the Fives can offer their gift of understanding. The Fives know, not from their careful observation, but from firsthand life experience, what it is like to feel awkward or ill at ease. The Fives know what it feels like to be confused or too scared to live life. This is the real gift of knowledge which the Fives can graciously share. In reaching out to others with understanding, the Fives, too, will come to life. For not only will they be alive mentally but also physically and emotionally. They will no longer be isolated from others or from other parts of themselves. When they step forward they will touch other human hearts. As Antoine de Saint-Exupéry wrote in *The Little Prince*: "It is only with the heart that one sees rightly. What is essential is invisible to the eye." The journey of the Fives will be to move out from that private space where they hold themselves and their possessions apart from others. As they move out, they will begin to let go of their inordinate desire for privacy and self-containment. This is the lifegrowth journey of the Fives, from the **passion of avarice** to the **virtue of detachment.**

THE SIXES

The word which captures the energy of the Sixes is **authority**. All the different varieties of Sixes in all different stages are always interacting with the world through their involvement with authority. However they attempt to fit into the world, it will always be in relationship to authority. Furthermore, the term "authority" will include anyone the Sixes decide should be included in that category. Their hypervigilance is always trained on authority.

In **compulsion** the Sixes react negatively to authority. The most obvious version of this is the rebel who makes a cause of butting up against whatever the authorities in life are promulgating. It's really not what they say, it's that they are in authority that is the real fighting issue. Another style of compulsive Six is the overly-dependent type. In this case, the Sixes will fret and worry but will always seek and follow the advice of an authority. The authority figure doesn't have to be the president of the country or the pastor at church. Besides these and other recognized authorities, it might also be a next door neighbor or a person who happens to be in front of them in line. These Sixes presume that everyone else knows more and better than they do. Even when they actually know something to be true, they will still ask someone else, "Are you sure?" They simply want to verify what they already know. A third style of Sixes includes those who make themselves into authorities. Whether or not they actually hold a position of authority doesn't matter. It's rather a case of assuming a parental approach to other people. These Sixes are fretful worriers, too. However, they don't ask for advice. They tell others what to do, how to be careful, what's "enough" and what's "too much." In compulsion their heavy reliance on being an authority to others is an attempt to quell the anxious fear of being uncertain. As the various Sixes focus all their energies on the outside authority, they lose all sense of themselves as gifted and faith-filled. Unless they accept the responsibility of their own uncertainty, they will never awaken to full life. Unless they learn to trust their own judgments, they will go on relying on others and counting noses.

In their most **gifted** state, the Sixes will believe in themselves and their ever-present gift of faith. They will understand that faith means to *believe* what we do not *know* for certain. In other words, to chase after rational certainty is to refuse to make the leap of faith. In their gifted state the Sixes realize that having the gift of faith allows them to live peacefully in the eye of the storm. It's as if they already have about them an instinct for what is and isn't so. They simply intuit what is transitory and differentiate it from what is permanent. They recognize the difference between truth and falsity, trustworthiness and trickery. They no longer need proof or verification. They won't need to insist on the agreement of all those around them. And they will be able to live with both certainty and uncertainty. When they learn to hear and accept the physical and emotional messages of their own persons, they will know that to feel anxiety is part of being human. And so they will no longer become anxious about being anxious. They will be more at peace with themselves and with the world. They will share the conviction of Lacordaire who said, "All I know of tomorrow is that Providence will rise before the sun." This peacefulness will offer a solid model for other anxious people. The Sixes will become interdependent with others, becoming a true friend, as they move from an overreliance on outer authority toward a new trust in their own inner authority. This is the lifegrowth journey of the Sixes as they move outward from the **passion of fear** to the **virtue of courage.**

THE SEVENS

One word which magnetizes the energy of the Sevens is **experience.** For them, life is a series of experiences. Through their senses, especially visual, they take in all the sensations that life offers. They revel in the sights, sounds, aromas, textures, flavors and stimulating ideas that abound in the world.

In the **compulsive** state the Sevens will seek to experience more and more different sensations. They will entertain in their heads a multitude of ideas and plans for the future. They will jump around in their conversations from one topic to another, telling stories about this idea, that plan or some event. They usually are great conversationalists who can talk about anything and everything. They will also hop around in their activities from one event to another and from one life plan to another. Sometimes this change will take place in a matter of moments with no backward glances. In compulsion, this rush to experience everything is actually a feverish escape from the pain and problems they hope to avoid in life. This carousel approach to life will continue until they have spent themselves or have had a shockingly negative experience that will awaken them.

In their most **gifted** state, the Sevens learn that the one true experience of life is the joy of being fully human and fully alive. They come to understand the difference between sensual experience and true joy. True joy is to celebrate every moment of life just as it comes to us. It is not the counterfeit creation of stimulating experiences. As John of the Cross said, "Joy is the echo of God's life in us." And, of course, God's life is always in us at every moment. When the Sevens wake up to recognize their innate giftedness, they will savor and digest each new moment without having to create an experience a minute. They will not continually collect options to ward off the panic of boredom. They will not have to keep moving to stay free. Without the frantic rush in their lives, there will be time and space for a deeper involvement with the things, ideas and people in their lives. They now distinguish a "good life" from "good times." They will no longer live on the surface of life but will penetrate the deep recesses of what it means to be fully human and fully alive. They will also be able to listen to more than just their own busy heads and plans. Increased awareness of the body will help to unlock the buried treasure of emotions within. They will finally recognize what John Powell says, "Happiness is an inside job. And true happiness comes to us as a byproduct of sharing our giftedness with others." When the Sevens, with their knowledge of both joy and pain, move to embrace others who are in pain, they will experience the truest joy of togetherness. This is the lifegrowth journey of the Sevens as they move from the **passion of gluttony** to the **virtue of sobriety.**

THE EIGHTS

The word which best embodies the energies of the Eights is **struggle.** The Eights are intensely involved with the world around them and all that is a part of it. One thing is constant with the Eights, their strong energy is forceful and interactive.

In **compulsion** the Eights will push the limits and boundaries of all situations and all the people they meet. One day they clearly carve out their territory, and it will be spacious. Then the next day they may carve boundaries even more broad. Eights can walk into any area and physically take command of the space just by the way they stand, or glance around. Or they may acquire command of the outer areas of the whole room in a slow and deliberate manner. They are instinctively creating a safe-zone for themselves. At the same time, they are letting others know it would be unwise to invade their personal space. It's really quite simple. It's really about self-preservation. It's very clear and forcefully direct. There's no mistaking the process. If others try to engage compulsed Eights, they will be cut off mercilessly. "No" is usually the first response from an Eight to a request of any kind. After the "No" may come efforts to reengage, but always with the Eight in charge of the process. Whatever might be offered by another will usually be debunked or belittled. It's not like criticism which picks at something you've said or done. It's just a quick, broad swipe which clears the deck. All this forceful wrestling is done by the compulsive Eights in order to avoid the discovery of their own weak and tender core. To protect their vulnerability and prevent being cut-off, they ironically create a climate which causes others to flee. It will most likely take a major negative event or a group confrontation, something with the force of a sledge hammer, to shake up and wake up the Eights.

In their most **gifted** state, the Eights will use their personal force to protect, defend and forge new ground. They will protect and defend the weak and defenseless who are suffering under the domination of others. They instinctively sense both sides of that equation: weakness and strength. They will use their force to push aside the corrupt institutions of society and thereby create a bold new world. In August of 1991, Boris Yeltsin, as president of Russia, stood atop a tank and defiantly denounced those who were attempting to take over the government, end the democratic processes and turn back toward totalitarianism. When he did this he was demonstrating the magnanimous, forceful, constructive ability of the Eights. Factually speaking, he was simply a 60-year-old, white-haired man, standing on a piece of machinery 6 feet high with no assurance of protection, shouting to a mob of people in the street: "Come, defend Russia!" However, in the reality of Russian and world history, he was a strong and forceful leader who courageously scaled the walls of the mighty enemy. He stood atop the enemy's armored parapet and to the whole world claimed victory for those who had been in slavery for 70 years. It was a bold gamble which in the moment seemed ludicrous. Here was the leader of Russia standing against the Soviet government, the Soviet Army, the KGB and the national police. However, the lives of everyone in Russia, the whole Soviet Union and all throughout the world were changed radically in that moment. This is how the gifted force of the Eights can forge a new life for others. The strong physical presence of their very persons can alter events large and small. The Eights' own concealed tenderness is touched and moved to action by the plight of others too weak to speak for themselves. Their lifegrowth journey will take them from the **passion of lust** to the **virtue of innocence.**

THE NINES

The word that most typifies the Nines' energy is **stable.** The Nines are like the great wonders of nature which remain generally the same, in season and out. The oceans, even with high tides and low, still remain the same large bodies of water. "Ole Man River keeps on rollin' along." And the Grand Canyon just sits there getting more grand every year.

In **compulsion** the Nines become the immovable object. All their energy is concentrated on not being moved, not being disturbed or upset. They minimize all that comes their way in life: tragedies, triumphs, loves and hates. These are all the same, just ordinary events which make up life. They come and they go, but life goes on. If it isn't this, it's that. The Nines make molehills out of other peoples' mountains. They say things like: "It's no big deal." "Why bother?" "It doesn't matter." "It makes no difference." "Don't bother me." "I don't want to be a bother." "Whatever you say is O.K." Sometimes their response is a simple shrug of the shoulders or movement of the chin. Translation: "I don't care." They speak in a matter-of-fact way, in a monotone voice, with no variation of intonations among the various words and sounds. All are the same. They like to keep everything in their lives the same. Their work and friends, their routine and possessions, everything and all relationships may for decades remain unchanged. If these maneuvers are not enough to keep outside or inside forces neutralized, the Nines will use TV, sleep, food, drugs, anything to anesthetize them from life and its changing energies. They resist the shifting sands of time. In compulsion, they are seeking a false harmony with themselves, others, and with the world. The Nines hold to the conviction that if they don't let anything disturbing get to their core, then they can maintain what they mistakenly think of as peace. Their compulsion has not only kept the world at bay, but it has caused them to lose touch with their own personal reality. They are no longer living in complete contact with reality. They are walking in a dreamlike sleep. They live in a pretend world which they have created. It is a sort of bubble uncontaminated by real life. It oftentimes takes a major shock or many good friends to jolt a Nine into wakefulness.

In their most **gifted** state, the Nines will awaken to the realization that to be fully alive they must actively become a person. This means loving themselves enough to care about who they are and how they are treated by others. They will develop and express their preferences. They will allow the vital stirrings within them to be made known as their own wants and needs. They will allow themselves to love others enough to engage them. They will love life enough to become constructively active in it day by day. They will hear the challenge in the words of John of the Cross: "In the evening of life we shall be judged by love." For the Nines to love is to be actively involved in all of life. In their giftedness, the Nines will allow the dynamic energies of change to bubble in turmoil within them and know that this is the lifegrowth journey they are meant to take. As they recognize the life-promoting value of discord in the stirrings of life, they will also look upon interpersonal discord in a new way. What was before a disagreement will now become a common brainstorming session. The fights of yesterday will be seen as the encounters of intimacy today. Through experience they will learn the life-giving energy of discord. There is a most basic process of physics that we can see any day in our kitchens which demonstrates this idea. When you take ice from the refrigerator it begins to melt, change from a solid into a liquid. When you place heat beneath a pan of water it will eventually change the water into air bubbles and then into the vapor of steam. All new life comes from rearranging the stable elements. With their natural sense of discord, the Nines can bring their true gift of harmony into the world. In their giftedness they will instinctively recognize that true harmony results from allowing disturbance and then sensitively weaving the disparate elements into a new fabric. Here we see the stability of the Nines take on a new sound. To life's happenings they no longer respond: "It's O.K. Calm down. It's no big deal." Rather, we hear them say: "It's O.K. Let's calm down. We can work it out together." This is the lifegrowth journey of the Nines as they move from the **passion of indifference** to the **virtue of action**.

ON THE LIFEGROWTH JOURNEY

Throughout our lives we will all experience some times of compulsion and other times of giftedness. When we are in our compulsive state, there will be moments when we feel driven, compelled to do or say this or that. We will think that we can't help being the way we are. We just have to!

We express this compulsivity by saying things like this:
"I've got to do it. No one else will!"
"I've got to be of help!"
"I've got to succeed!"
"I've got to be in the mood!"

"I've got to have more time to get ready!"

"I've got to know what I'm supposed to do!"

"I've got to be free and have my options!"

"I've got to be in charge!"

"I've got to have peace at any price!"

It's as if we're trapped in a certain style of behavior. We seem to be blinded to the fact that there are other ways to view life and interact with reality. We all get compulsive at times, sometimes for a moment or perhaps for many years. The times of compulsion come and go throughout our lives. The more internal and external stress we have, the greater will be our tendency to live in compulsion. However, the more we become aware of our compulsiveness and the stress which provokes it, the more we will be able to open to our giftedness.

When we are open to our giftedness a new ease will be apparent in our interactions with others. The passions will give way to the virtues within us and our gift will flow freely. We will not feel as though we are forcing something to happen in a certain way. We won't be hearing ourselves say: "I've got to . . . !" We will be empathic toward others and their different ways of being. And we will be collaborative with others in combining our gifts for the greatest good of all. The Ones will be guides, not judges. The Twos will be nurturing not smothering. The Threes will be encouraging not grandstanding. The Fours will sensitively listen to others, not be self-absorbed. The Fives will be open and assertive, not private and in hiding. The Sixes will be relaxed good friends, not deferential worry-warts or feisty daredevils. The Sevens will be interesting companions, not flighty partygoers. The Eights will be tender and warm, not tough and combative. The Nines will be assertive and loving, not passive and neglectful. We will not be trying to cover the gift with an imitation. Rather we will let go of our compulsions and simply let our gifts flow freely.

In order for you to be able to identify with one or another of the Numbers that you have read about in this chapter, both the compulsion and the giftedness should resonate in you. It's easy enough for any of us to claim the giftedness part. That looks and sounds really good in the case of any of the various Numbers. However, if you can see and hear yourself described in the compulsive state, too, then you have really found yourself.

SELF-OBSERVATION JOURNAL:

One way to identify both your passion of compulsion and your virtue of giftedness is to recognize where you invest your energies. Using the figure shown below, try to decide in which area you focus most of your physical, emotional and spiritual energies.

If none of the descriptions in this Chapter resonate with you yet, remember, this is a journey. Be patient, compassionate and understanding with yourself.

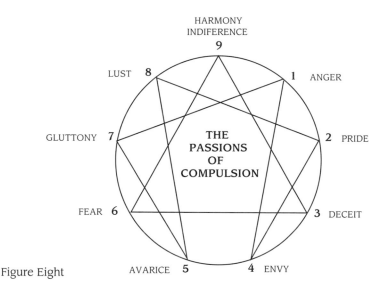

Figure Eight

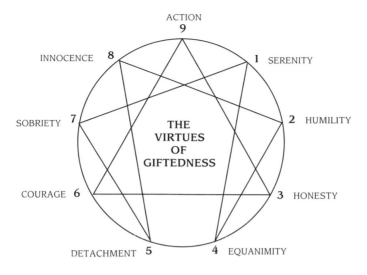

Figure Nine

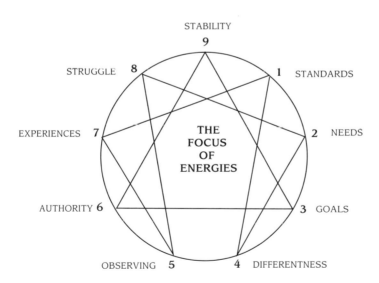

Figure Ten

CHAPTER TEN

Wings and Arrows and Other Fun Things

THE WINGS

You can't be around the Enneagram for long without hearing about wings and arrows. First, let's look at the wings. What are these wings? I like to think of them as I do my neighbors. I don't "live" in the houses on either side of me. But they are very familiar to me. Sometimes I visit there for a while. When I'm there, I act a little bit like the permanent residents do rather than in my usual way of acting. Translated into Enneagram theory: The two Numbers on either side of our own Number on the Enneagram circle are our wings. For example, the Number One has Nine on one side and Two on the other. So for the Ones, the wings will be Nine and Two. We always remain the Number we are from the beginning, but there can be influences from other sources that give added layers to our persons. The wings are among these influences.

For example, a Number One is a very principled person. Let's say that in a certain Number One we know there seems to be a strong influence from the Two wing.

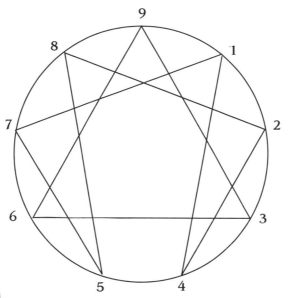

Figure Eleven

In that case, one of the principles that will likely be important to this particular One will be involvement in **helping people** as the Twos do. With another Number One there may be a stronger influence from the Nine wing. This may draw the Number One more toward **fixing the world**, perhaps working to clean up the environment. Both Ones are highly principled and work hard to do good. But the influence of each wing defines that good in different ways.

For another example, let's look at the Six. When the influence is strongest from the Seven wing, we will encounter a rather playful Six. However, if the influence is coming predominantly from the Five wing, then we will see a more serious, perhaps even an overwhelmingly shy and withdrawn person. In these examples we see only one wing influencing the Number while the other wing seems not to be very well developed. I tend to think both wings can be influential and will exert that influence at different times in our lives. In any case, it is good to keep the wings in mind when looking for your Number. Perhaps you will find that two or three consecutive Numbers keep sounding like you. You may have actually found your Number plus your wings.

OTHER INFLUENCES

Whatever our Enneagram Number is, it will be affected by other sources of influence. Among the possible influences I would include are our parents, our brothers and sisters, birth order, nationality and economic levels, the neighborhood where we grew up, the schools we attended, the teachers and friends we knew as youngsters, as well as all our major life events. These influences tend to shape and affect our original personalities. They won't change our basic position on the Enneagram, but they will lend layers of unique color and texture to the basic description of the Number. For example, consider a Number Five who grew up as an only child in a comfortable home with strict parents of German and English backgrounds. Today, he is a quiet, reserved person who works as a scientific researcher. Another Five grew up in a large, outgoing Irish and Italian family in the middle of a big city. Today, she teaches group therapy at a city college. The many differences between these two Fives are probably the result of the special influences which overlay their basic Five tendencies.

Here is something else to consider in locating your Enneagram Number. Observe yourself to determine how much of your behavior is still dictated by so-called "parent tapes," by what your parents modeled for you, asked or told you to do. You may find the overlay of your parents' Numbers obscuring your own. A very dutiful, responsible Six I once knew thought she was a Four for a while. You see, she had been trying to follow the suggestions of her mother. Her mother was a Four who wanted the daughter to be a poet and to dress artistically. The daughter never really "got it." She didn't interiorize her mother's artistry. She just did what her mother had told her to do. As you search for your Number, remember there may be "other" influences at work in you. So be aware of the influence of these various overlays.

THE ARROWS OR DIRECTIONS

The Enneagram figure is shown here with the arrows (see Figure 12). You can see that each Number has two lines running between it and two other Numbers. The lines, you will notice, have arrows on them. This figure represents the arrow theory. There are various presentations of this theory. In most of these presentations, the line with the *arrow leading away* from your Number is considered to be the destructive or unhealthy direction for you to go. The line with the *arrow leading toward* your Number is said to be your direction for growth.

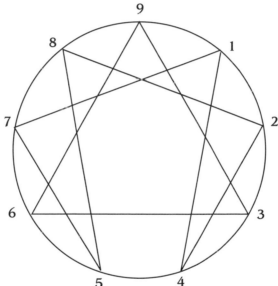

Figure Twelve

For example, notice that the Number Two has lines connecting it to the Number Four and to the Number Eight. The line with the *arrow leading toward* the Two connects the Two with the Four. This signifies that it is healthy for the Two to take into itself some of the positive Four behaviors. For instance, it would be good for the Twos to be more introspective in order to identify their own needs. However, the line with the *arrow leading away* from the Two connects the Two with the Eight. This signifies that it is unhealthy when the Two moves into the negative behaviors of the Eight.

How does all this affect you now? You are probably still on that part of your journey which is the search for your Number. Stay with your search and don't rush yourself. Much farther on the journey you will become more involved with the movement around the Enneagram circle. However, for now you may want to know that there are two directions, two other positions on the Enneagram circle that may feel familiar to you. Their behaviors may seem a bit like your own at times.

So now you are still searching for your Number, but you will also be on the lookout for two other Numbers that meet yours by way of the directional lines. Then, of course, there are the two wings we spoke of earlier on either side of your Number. They also have an influence on you. Remember, you are who you are from the beginning, one Number from start to finish. But now you see you will have some special relationship to four other Numbers. Confused? Try only this one example: You may be identifying with the Number Two at this point. If so, your wings will be One and Three. Your directions will be Eight and Four. It will not be surprising if something about all those Numbers seems familiar to you.

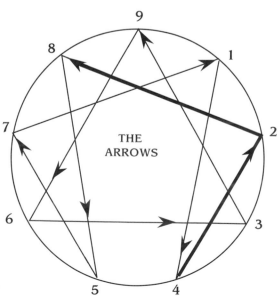

Figure Thirteen

NOW FOR THE FUN

In the following pages there will be several situations suggested. After reading the description of each situation, consider what your response would be. Then read the examples of how each Number might typically look, behave or respond to the situation described. Compare your response to the examples given for each Number. Perhaps you will find yourself in these pages.

LEAVIN' ON A JET PLANE

Suppose you're going on an extended trip to another country. Money, language and vacation time from work are not problems for you. Under those circumstances what country would you choose to live in for six months? What would attract you? And, why?

Take a few minutes to consider your choice of country and the reasons. Now compare your choice with the possibilities given here.

> *The Number One:* I would definitely visit England. The plays are exquisite, the people are so very proper. And the universities there are of the highest standard. It would be so inspiring to visit Parliament where the principles of modern Western democracy were first enunciated.

> *The Number Two:* I would love to visit Italy. The people are so warm and welcoming. In the restaurants you are taken care of so well. The Italians act like they had set the table just waiting for you to come. I would feel so at home with people like that.

> *The Number Three:* I'm on my way to Singapore. This is an up-and-coming place. The manufacturing center has effectively implemented the latest ideas of a market economy. I'd like to get a handle on what they're doing and how it might enhance my future business goals. Besides, they have the best tours of the Orient leaving from there.

The Number Four: France would be my choice. The ballet, the art museums, the cuisine and the incomparable countryside are unique. I would like to get a studio or perhaps a country house, some place that could provide the mood and atmosphere for me to do my writing and painting. Paris is the artistic center of the world. C'est magnifique!

The Number Five: I think I would choose to live in Luxembourg. It's a small, quiet place that was in the center of World War II. Today it is the hub of European finance. It would be a good central location from which to travel. It would be very interesting for me to travel all around the world just to see it and to learn about the many different cultures.

The Number Six: Germany is where I think I should go. My friends said I would like to live and work there because it's very orderly and the people are good workers, very responsible and loyal. I think I would appreciate the respect for tradition and the camaraderie of the German lifestyle.

The Number Seven: Australia is filled with possibilities for fun: boating, kangaroos, koalas, surfing and deep sea fishing, hiking in the outback. Wow! There are so many options. I hear the people are very friendly and have a great zest for life. This sounds terrific to me.

The Number Eight: One country's not enough for me. I need a whole continent. And I would go to Africa. First I'd go directly to Morocco for the gambling and night life. Then I would go to the East African Coast for the grand scenery. While I'm there I will go on a Safari in Kenya. Finally, I'll rent a boat and sail the open seas to Madagascar.

The Number Nine: Traveling sounds like so much trouble, too much activity. I guess I'd go to the Caribbean on a cruise and spend lots of time lounging on the boat or beach. Then I would continue the cruise all around South America. Whenever I got to a country that felt comfortable for me I would stay there.

Did the flavor of any of these excursions compare with your travel plans?

USING COLORS TO SYMBOLIZE

Choose colors for each of the Numbers that symbolically represent certain qualities of each. Now compare your listing of colors and qualities with the list given here. They don't have to be exactly the same. Just see if you have captured some of the qualities of each Number. Enjoy!

The Number One:	Silver is so pure and clean.
The Number Two:	Pink is warm and inviting.
The Number Three:	Gold—go for the gold!
The Number Four:	Mauve is most unusual.
The Number Five:	Deep blue is secret and rich.
The Number Six:	Beige goes with everything. It's dependable.
The Number Seven:	Bright green suggests new life.
The Number Eight:	Red is bold and forthright.
The Number Nine:	Yellow is warm and comforting like the sun.

RISE AND SHINE

What motivates you to get up in the morning when it is not a regular work day? It's a free day. To locate a response to this question may take you some time and require several days or even weeks of self-observation. Eventually compare your response to the possibilities given here.

The Number One:	There's too much to be done to stay in bed.
The Number Two:	I want to get breakfast for the others.
The Number Three:	I can't wait to get started accomplishing things.
The Number Four:	When I feel in the right mood, when the spirit moves me, then I'll get up.
The Number Five:	When I think of something interesting I want to read or learn about, then I suddenly just get up.
The Number Six:	I get up because that's what a person is supposed to do, isn't it?
The Number Seven:	Everyday is a new adventure. The sun is shining somewhere.
The Number Eight:	Whenever I get up is when the day starts. That's all there is to it.
The Number Nine:	Oh, it's so hard every day, but especially when it's a free day. The pillow and I were made for each other. But if I smell the coffee or breakfast cooking, this will rouse me.

THE OLYMPIC COMMITTEE

Imagine that nine different people, one person of each Enneagram Number, are chosen to serve on an Olympic Committee. Together they will plan and prepare for the next Olympic Games. All of them will choose jobs according to their special gifts.

Take some time to consider what job you would choose and why. Then compare your choice with the possibilities given here.

The Number One:

"I want to see that all the preparations are done right. I would like these Olympics to be in keeping with the highest standards of the original Olympic principles. So, I will choose to monitor all the processes to be sure we meet the ideal."

The Number Two:

"When I think of all those young athletes coming so far from their homes and being under such stress, my heart goes out to them. I would like to make them feel at home. So, I will choose to arrange all the accommodations to meet the athletes' every need. And I will also arrange to feed them all, especially their favorite foods."

The Number Three:

"The Olympic Games are the biggest world event of the year. We want everyone to hear about it and know it's the place to be. Our goal in preparing should be to get as many people as possible involved and excited about this upcoming event. I will organize and lead the program to market the Games to the media, to the business community and to every man, woman and child in every home. We'll make the Olympics the place everyone wants to be."

The Number Four:

"The Olympic Games have such profound significance. They symbolize the world family joining for play and competition, for pageantry and community. I would very much like to create the opening and closing ceremonies which will speak to the whole world of these great themes. I hope the presentations will be truly distinctive and poetic expressions of the communal soul of humanity."

The Number Five:

"I was thinking that much of our preparatory work cannot be done before we gather certain information and set up some systems for how to proceed. We will have to know the demographics: How many are expected to attend? How many men? How many women? How many children and of what ages? How will they travel here? How long will be the average stay? There are scores of questions to be answered. It would be fascinating for me to take on the job of researching the information and setting up the needed systems."

The Number Six:

"I know that when I'm planning to go to a big event like this I'm worried about all the things I don't know yet. I usually want to get the directions clear, maybe even have a map. I want to know the schedule and fees for all the events. I would like to know beforehand where I'll be staying and how to get to other places in the area. I will take the job of preparing maps, schedules, guidebooks and maybe even setting up informations booths, security teams and emergency stations to help those who come to the Games."

The Number Seven:

"The Olympics are games! They're supposed to be fun. They're athletic contests, sure, but it's really a great big party for the world. I want to plan a party atmosphere that lights up the whole Olympic Village: eateries, bistros, sidewalk musicians and magicians, loads of fun for everyone. In fact, we could make our committee meetings enjoyable, too. I'll bring wine and cheese to these gatherings and to your subcommittee meetings, too, if you want."

The Number Eight:

"There's not going to be any great big event unless we get started on the building of the Olympic Village. I'll take this on. I can work with these construction companies and the trade unions as well. I'll keep them in line. And I'll work with the politicians and financial backers besides. I'll get it all done. And I'll see to it that nobody cheats us. I'll make them get it done on time and under cost."

The Number Nine:

"There are so many different parts to this whole process. Each of you has your separate part. Then there will be all the various countries and their different requests. We have to pull this all together into a unified whole. You have all been asking me to take this on, so I guess I will. I'll chair our committee. I'll try to work things out among all of us so we don't upset one another while we work together. And I guess I'll be the one to smooth things over between the countries, too. If you all think I'm the one for this job, I'll give it a try."

Wouldn't this be a rich group of people? They are filled with diverse talents, and yet as a unified whole, they can provide all that's necessary for a wonderful Olympic Games. Of course, this is possible with any group of people who understand and celebrate one anothers' gifts. To value others' differentness is one of the great by-products of learning the Enneagram.

As you can see from the playful examples used in this chapter, the Enneagram of personal motivation can be applied to any part of our lives. The Numbers we are will indicate the motivational levels which permeate our lives. What we choose to do and say, how we relate to the world and interact with others—all this comes from the specific motivations of whatever Numbers we are.

CHAPTER ELEVEN

Self-Observation and Self-Remembering

SELF-OBSERVATION

All throughout this book there has been repeated encouragements to develop the habit of self-observation. If you recall in Chapter Three, this was described as the process of developing our own inner observer. The idea is to develop the ability to observe ourselves at the same time that we are living life. When we first began to do this, we may have felt so self-conscious that we stopped living to some extent and became an observer of life. This usually happens in the early stages of the learning process. However, if we stayed with it, by now we have probably moved along to where we can observe ourselves even as we are actively involved with life.

This activity of observation is usually what psychotherapists do for us. They observe us: our feelings, our actions, what we say and how we relate. Then they are able to suggest things about us that we don't seem to know. As a psychotherapist, I can honestly say that we don't really know more nor can we see through people. We simply have a better vantage point and a way to make sense out of what we observe. We are observing from the outside at a distance from the personality. Therefore, we can see more clearly than the person who is on the inside of the same personality. However, if we develop our own inner observer, we can tell ourselves a great deal about who we really are—from the inside.

SELF-REMEMBERING

Who we really are, under the cover, is the original core of our persons. It is at this core that the full giftedness is hidden under the protective layers of personality. The more self-observation we are able to do, the more we will remember of the original self. This self-remembering effect is the second of two legs on which Gurdjieff built his Enneagram work. He taught that developing the habit of self-observation was the necessary prelude to self-remembering. Self-remembering is becoming aware of ourselves in ways that capture the whole experience of being who we are. Remembering implies putting the members of the whole back together again. We become aware of what we're thinking and how we feel. We are also aware of the sensations of our bodies and a sense of where we are in space in relation to others. Self-remembering does not involve doing anything about this awareness but simply calls for being aware of ourselves on all these levels at once. When we can remember ourselves in this way, bringing the various parts of our whole selves back together again, then our giftedness can flow freely. Using the earlier image of the rosebush, when we remove the protective rose cone, the leaves grow, the flowers bloom and their aroma fills the air. The original gift of the rosebush flows freely.

As we experience this process of self-remembering, two different kinds of feelings will probably occur. One feeling gives us a very pleasant sense of coming home to ourselves. As someone said to me, "It's like connecting the dots in a child's puzzle book and suddenly you recognize a familiar picture you had long forgotten." This feeling is usually associated with the first part of the original gift. The other feeling will be unpleasant at first. It will come to us as we gradually open to and own our avoidances. This is the second part of the gift, the part we tried so long and so hard to keep hidden. Again, as someone once said to me, "I recognized this part of me for sure. It's what I had spent years of time and energy trying to hide. Strangely, though, it was like meeting an old friend." Many people report feeling relief when the masquerade finally ends. Eventually we will come to embrace this part of ourselves, too. It is, after all, the part of ourselves which will lead us on the next path of the lifegrowth journey.

We have met ourselves in bits and pieces along the journey. Now let's bring those bits and pieces together. It's time to see the whole, complete person according to each Enneagram Number. The remaining pages of this chapter have been designed for you to do some self-observation. All that has been described about each Number is summarized. Then a list of words which help to describe each Number is given. The words have been carefully arranged to demonstrate the progression we all are capable of: going gradually from giftedness at the top into compulsion at the bottom. As you read down each page, use your developing self-observation process. Try to stay open to seeing yourself in the best possible light as well as in the worst possible darkness. In other words, try to say to yourself: "What is the best version of me I am capable of being and what is the worst version, the one that I would like most to hide?" This effort at total openness will help greatly in identifying yourself in the pages that follow.

NUMBER ONE

THE GIFT: An instinct for **completion and perfection** and a sense of incompletion and limitation
THE CENTER: The Gut-Instinct Center: *Loss* provokes *anger* "I was not good enough."
IDEALIZED SELF-IMAGE: "I am right and good and in control of myself."
AVOIDANCE: Incompletion and Limitation
DEFENSE MECHANISM: Reaction Formation
ENERGY FOCUS: on Standards
VIRTUE OF GIFTEDNESS: Serenity
PASSION OF COMPULSION: Anger/Resentment

IN GIFTEDNESS

PRINCIPLED   CONSCIENTIOUS   NOBLE   FAIR   ETHICAL

JUST   RIGHT   MORAL   DISCIPLINED   GOOD   CRUSADER

IDEALIST HARD WORKER   PRECISE ADMITS MISTAKES   GOOD MODEL

TOLERANT   STRICT CONSCIENCE   TIRELESS   PROPER   PURIST

REFORMER   CONTROLLED

NON-ADAPTABLE   CRITICAL

APPROPRIATE   IMPERSONAL

1

TENSE   RIGID   PREACHES

JUDGMENTAL   CONTROLLING

INFLEXIBLE   ABRASIVE   SCOLDING   PURITANICAL   INTOLERANT

OBSTINATE   ANGRY DOGMATIC OPINIONATED   OBSESSIVE THOUGHTS

SEVERE   RESENTFUL   SELF-RIGHTEOUS   INDIGNANT   PUNITIVE

IN COMPULSION

NUMBER TWO

THE GIFT: A natural feel for **caring and nurturing** and for noticing neediness.
THE CENTER: The Emotion-Motion Center: *Loss* provokes *anxiety* about past *rejection* for being *defective*.
"I was too needy."
IDEALIZED SELF-IMAGE: "I care only about you and your needs."
AVOIDANCE: Own neediness
DEFENSE MECHANISM: Repression
ENERGY FOCUS: on Needs
VIRTUE OF GIFTEDNESS: Humility
PASSION OF COMPULSION: Pride

IN   GIFTEDNESS

NURTURING   WARM   FEELS OTHER'S NEEDS   COMPASSIONATE   CARING

CONCERNED   TENDER   LOVING   ATTENTIVE   HUMBLE   GIVING

HELPFUL   SYMPATHETIC   AWWWWH!   GENEROUS   AFFIRMING

PHYSICALLY TOUCHING   APPRECIATIVE   COMPANION   THOUGHTFUL

INTIMATE   EMOTIONAL

CATERING   EFFUSIVE

INTRUSIVE   PRIDEFUL

FLATTERER   **2**   PATRONIZING

IMPORTANT TO OTHERS   FALSE HUMILITY

INDISPENSIBLE   REPRESSES OWN NEEDS

SMOTHERING   NEEDS TO BE NEEDED   FEELS UNAPPRECIATED

RESCUER   MARTYR-VICTIM-GUILT PRODUCER   MANIPULATOR

POSSESSIVE   REPRESSES AGGRESSIVE FEELINGS   DOMINATING

IN   COMPULSION

NUMBER THREE

THE GIFT: A keen feel for **making and producing** as well as recognizing the **void of nothingness.**
THE CENTER: The Emotion-Motion Center: *Loss* provokes *anger* about past *rejection* for being *defective*.
"There was nothing to me."
IDEALIZED SELF-IMAGE: "I am productive and successful."
AVOIDANCE: Nothingness/Failure
DEFENSE MECHANISM: Identification
ENERGY FOCUS: on Goals
VIRTUE OF GIFTEDNESS: Honesty
PASSION OF COMPULSION: Deceit

IN GIFTEDNESS

SUCCESSFUL   ADMIRED   PRODUCTIVE   ENERGETIC   OUTSTANDING

ACCOMPLISHER   GOAL-ORIENTED   PRACTICAL   EFFICIENT   CONFIDENT

POSITIVE   SELF-STARTER   ENCOURAGER   PROGRESSIVE   SOCIAL

ACHIEVER   MOTIVATOR   SELF-ASSURED   COMPETENT

GOT IT ALL TOGETHER   CAREER FOCUSED

COMPETITIVE   PRAGMATIC

IMPRESSIVE   AMBITIOUS

IMAGE CONSCIOUS   EXPEDIENT

PLAYS ROLES   PRESTIGE CONSCIOUS

SEEKS ATTENTION AND ADMIRATION   PRETENTIOUS   SELF-PROMOTING

LACKS SELF-AWARENESS   CHAMELEON   ARROGANT   SELF-DECEPTIVE

EXPLOITATIVE   CALCULATING   OPPORTUNISTIC   HOSTILE WHEN IGNORED

IN COMPULSION

NUMBER FOUR

THE GIFT: A sensitivity for **uniqueness** and a feel for **commonness.**
THE CENTER: The Emotion-Motion Center: Loss provokes anxiety about past *rejection* for being *defective.*
"I was too common."
IDEALIZED SELF-IMAGE: "I am unique . . . different."
AVOIDANCE: Commonness/Ordinariness
DEFENSE MECHANISM: Artistic Sublimation
ENERGY FOCUS: on Differentness
VIRTUE OF GIFTEDNESS: Equanimity
PASSION OF COMPULSION: Envy

IN GIFTEDNESS

UNIQUE   AESTHETIC   SELF-AWARE   PERSONAL   REVEALING

ARTISTICALLY EXPRESSIVE   CHERISHES BEAUTY INTUITIVE INSPIRED

VULNERABLE   EMOTIONALLY TOUCHES OTHERS   HONEST ABOUT SELF

ORIGINAL   IMAGINATIVE   AUTHENTIC   ELEGANT   DISTINCTIVE

SENSITIVE   INDIVIDUALIST

UNUSUAL   CLASSY

FEELS DIFFERENT   **4**   SPECIAL

ENIGMATIC   EXQUISITE

ROMANTIC   AFFECTED

FLAMBOYANT   NOSTALGIC   SELF-INHIBITING   FANTASIZES

DEPRESSIVE FEARS SUCCESS ENVIOUS   SELF-ABSORBED

MELANCHOLIC   SELF-PITYING   IMPRACTICAL   MOODY ALIENATED

TORMENTED HOPELESS SELF-REPROACHFUL   DESPAIRING

IN COMPULSION

NUMBER FIVE

THE GIFT: A knowledge about **knowing** and not **knowing.**
THE CENTER: The Cognitive Center: *Loss* provokes *fear* about past *abandonment* for being *found lacking.*
"I didn't know enough."
IDEALIZED SELF-IMAGE: "I am knowledgeable."
AVOIDANCE: Not knowing
DEFENSE MECHANISM: Isolation and Compartmentalization
ENERGY FOCUS: on Observing
VIRTUE OF GIFTEDNESS: Detachment
PASSION OF COMPULSION: Avarice

IN   GIFTEDNESS

KNOWLEDGEABLE   OBSERVANT   THOROUGH   PERCEPTIVE   WISE

PROFOUND   INTERESTING   CURIOUS   INSIGHTFUL   OBJECTIVE

ORIGINAL THINKER   KEEPS CONFIDENCES   SPECULATIVE   RESEARCHER

NON-THREATENING   UNDERSTANDING   GENTLE   INTERESTED   EXPERT

CRYPTIC   DROLL HUMOR

LITERAL   SELF-CONTAINED

PRIVATE   CONCENTRATED

INVISIBLE   UNINVOLVED

SELF-RELIANT   INTENSE

WITHDRAWS   DETERMINED

GUARDS AGAINST INTRUSION   DISTANT   ABSORBED IN THOUGHT

ISOLATES FEELINGS   EASILY OVERWHELMED   CYNICAL   ECCENTRIC

RECLUSIVE   DESPONDENT   IMMOBILIZED   HOARDS   NIHILIST

IN   COMPULSION

NUMBER SIX

THE GIFT: A knowledge of **faith** and **uncertainty**.
THE CENTER: The Cognitive Center: *Loss* provokes *fear* about past *abandonment* for being *found lacking.*
"I wasn't faithful enough."
IDEALIZED SELF-IMAGE: "I am cooperative: dutiful, loyal and responsible."
AVOIDANCE: Uncertainty
DEFENSE MECHANISM: Projection
ENERGY FOCUS: on Authority
VIRTUE OF GIFTEDNESS: Courage
PASSION OF COMPULSION: Fear

IN GIFTEDNESS

LOYAL   DEPENDABLE   RELIABLE   HONORABLE   DUTIFUL   DEDICATED

TRUSTING   UPHOLDS AUTHORITY   STRONG BONDER   TRUSTWORTHY

ENDEARING   COMMITTED   ENGAGING   FAITHFUL   ORDERLY

RESPONSIBLE   TRUE FRIEND   INTERDEPENDENT   GOOD WORKER

VIGILANT   PLEASER

COOPERATIVE   COMPLIANT

TEASER   REACTIVE

RULE FOLLOWER   INDECISIVE

SEEKS PERMISSION   SEEKS APPROVAL

AMBIVALENT CONTRADICTORY WORRIER   BLAMER   CAUTIOUS OR DAREDEVIL

INFERIORITY   EVASIVE   DEPENDENT OR REBELLIOUS

ARGUMENTATIVE   EASILY RATTLED   PHOBIC

DEAD SURE OR DOUBTFUL   PARANOID   COWARDLY

IN COMPULSION

NUMBER SEVEN

THE GIFT: A knowledge of the heights of **joy** and the depths of **sadness.**

THE CENTER: The Cognitive Center: *Loss* provokes *fear* about past *abandonment* for being *found lacking.*

"I wasn't happy enough."

IDEALIZED SELF-IMAGE: "I am happy and life is terrific."

AVOIDANCE: Sadness

DEFENSE MECHANISM: Intellectual Sublimation

ENERGY FOCUS: on Experience

VIRTUE OF GIFTEDNESS: Sobriety

PASSION OF COMPULSION: Gluttony

IN GIFTEDNESS

JOYFUL   GRATEFUL   ENTHUSIASTIC   DELIGHTFUL   TERRIFIC

SPONTANEOUS   EXUBERANT   VERSATILE   AMUSING

EXTROVERTED   MULTITALENTED   FUTURISTIC   NETWORKER

LIVELY   EXPERIENTIAL   HUMOROUS   SEEKS OPTIONS

APPRECIATOR   PLAYFUL   LIGHTHEARTED

SEEKS VARIETY   GREGARIOUS

PLANNER   7   SCATTERED

INCONSISTENT   INCOMPLETES

CHANGEABLE   NEEDS FREEDOM

HYPERACTIVE   IMPULSIVE   EXCESSIVE   DEMANDS IMMEDIATE

GRATIFICATION   MATERIALISTIC   FLITS   SENSATIONALIST

GLUTTONOUS   SEEKS ATTENTION   SUPERFICIAL   FEARS DEPTH

PANICS   ACTS OUT ANXIETY   RECKLESS   ESCAPIST

IN COMPULSION

NUMBER EIGHT

THE GIFT: A strong sense of **power** and **vulnerability/weakness.**
THE CENTER: The Gut-Instinct Center: *Loss* provokes *anger*
about past *separation* for being *bad or wrong.*
"I was weak and vulnerable."
IDEALIZED SELF-IMAGE: "I am invincible."
AVOIDANCE: Vulnerability/Weakness
DEFENSE MECHANISM: Denial
ENERGY FOCUS: on Struggle
VIRTUE OF GIFTEDNESS: Innocence
PASSION OF COMPULSION: Lust

IN   GIFTEDNESS

STRONG   SELF-ASSURED   CONFIDENT   POWERFUL

PROTECTIVE   INSPIRING   GRAND   STURDY

LEADER   DECISIVE   SURE   BUILDER   FIGHTS FOR FAIRNESS

DETERMINED   MAGNANIMOUS   CONSTRUCTIVE   ENTERPRISING

ADVOCATE   ASSERTIVE   EXPANSIVE   TAKES CHARGE

STRUGGLES   WRESTLES

FORCEFUL   PREVAILING

POWER BROKER   **8**   WILLFUL

BLUNT   FORTHRIGHT

CONTROLLING   ADVERSARIAL

DOMINEERING   IMPULSIVE   DEFICIENT   GRANDIOSE

CONFRONTATIONAL   INTIMIDATING   DESTRUCTIVE   EXPLOSIVE

RAGEFUL   RUTHLESS   ACTS OUT OF FEAR OF ATTACK   VENGEFUL

IN   COMPULSION

NUMBER NINE

THE GIFT: A strong instinct for **harmony** and a sense for **discord.**

THE CENTER: The Gut-Instinct Center: *Loss* provokes *anger* about past *separation* for being *bad or wrong.* "I disagreed."

IDEALIZED SELF-IMAGE: "I am easygoing and agreeable."

AVOIDANCE: Discord

DEFENSE MECHANISM: Narcotization

ENERGY FOCUS: on Stable

VIRTUE OF GIFTEDNESS: Action

PASSION OF COMPULSION: Indifference

IN   GIFTEDNESS

AGREEABLE   SETTLED   EASYGOING   CALM   RELAXED   STABLE

RECEPTIVE   SUPPORTIVE   GUILELESS   CONTENT   PATIENT

UNSELF-CONSCIOUS   GOOD NATURED   UNPRETENTIOUS   ACCEPTING

REASSURING   UNIFYING   PEACEFUL   ACCOMMODATING

PRESERVATIONIST   DOWN TO EARTH

SENSUAL   MINIMIZER

LAID BACK   **9**   SELF-EFFACING

DISTRACTED   FORGETFUL

COMPLACENT   INDIFFERENT

SELF-DEPRECATING   PASSIVE   RESIGNED   NON-RESPONSIVE

STUBBORN   FATALISTIC   SELF-NEGLECTFUL   DISENGAGED

EMOTIONALLY DISCONNECTED   PUNITIVE   OBSTINATE   OBLIVIOUS

IN COMPULSION

CHAPTER TWELVE

Continuing Your Enneagram Journey

FOR THOSE OF YOU STILL IN SEARCH OF YOUR NUMBER

From the start of our journey we have been involved in the activity of self-observation. This, as promised, will lead to greater self-awareness or self-remembering of the real and original person at the core. If you have come to this point in the book and have not yet been able to identify yourself as one of the Enneagram Numbers, please don't stop journeying. Keep searching, keep your self-observation practice active. It's not that it didn't work. It's just that you haven't yet gotten to where you need to get. Just as each of us is unique, we all experience different timing on this journey of growth. Besides continuing your self-observation, seek out other Enneagam sources. There are many good books and tapes in the bibliography that might be helpful.* There are probably workshops available in your area. Ask around. A live presentation of the Enneagram is most helpful for many people. It's one thing to read about the energies of each Number. However, seeing and hearing and experiencing these energies in a person standing before you will bring the message home to you most clearly.

*(*I am working on a new book myself to be titled* Finding Yourself on the Enneagram Circle. *It is designed to help extend this initial searching process.)*

FOR THOSE OF YOU WHO HAVE
FOUND THEIR NUMBER

A word to those of you whose journey has resulted in your finding yourself (your Number) in the Enneagram scheme. Don't rush to change yourself. Remember how the journey went from infancy to this point. We used all our energies to cover and thereby create a distance from our true selves. At the same time, we self-created a caricature of who we really are. Don't rush to do that again in a new way. You'll end up at the same dead-end.

ENJOY THE JOURNEY

Here are some suggestions to help you enjoy this part of the journey. Continue to self-observe. There is a page of questions at the end of this chapter which may be helpful for continuing your self-observation. Try some of these questions and make up others of your own. Take one question at a time and live with it for a while, a few days, a few weeks. See what discoveries you come to that you can relate to your journey. For example, take the concept of money. How do you feel about it, think about it, experience it, relate to it, use it, and so forth? Now how does what you find out about yourself and money expand your self-understanding? Again, don't rush yourself. Enjoy the process. Treat each new find as if it were a piece of a puzzle you just found under the game table. Remember you haven't been in conscious touch with many of these parts of yourself since you were a toddler. It's like reacquainting yourself with a long-lost friend, someone you once knew and loved dearly. That's one of the reasons this phase is referred to as self-remembering.

BE COMPASSIONATE WITH YOURSELF
AND OTHERS

Of course, you're going to find some pieces that you don't like or that might embarrass you or evoke a sense of shame. Love yourself as you would your best friend. Compassion means to suffer with or feel deeply another's misfortune. Be assured that who you are is simply who you are at this point in your journey. You have a wonderful opportunity now to get to know yourself at a deeper, more spiritual level than ever before. Don't put a self-imposed roadblock of judgment or recrimination on the path of your journey.

Extend the same compassion to others in your life. I've never met anyone with an interest in the Enneagram who doesn't try to "figure out" everyone else they know. First there are family and friends, then co-workers or other community members. And then—there are "those obnoxious people who drive us crazy." To say, don't use the Enneagram on others, just focus on yourself is like telling little children not to giggle. It's impossible for us to resist. As long as we're probably going to use it, here are a few hints. Don't force it on anyone who indicates they're not interested. Don't insist to someone else, "I've got your Number." In some cases long-standing friendships have cooled because of this. Remember that the Enneagram helps us to see beneath the cover. Recall, too, that the cover was first put in place to protect us from some threatening danger. Only the persons who put the covers in place to begin with will be able to decide when they can survive without them. Be a patient companion to others who are on the journey.

BRANCH OUT

Find other people who are also interested in the Enneagram. Get together regularly. Share your self-observations with each other. This is very helpful in the process of developing understanding and compassion for other views of reality. Read other Enneagram books in a group and share different reactions, insights and feelings. Together, use the various audio and video tapes which are available. Be companions to one another on the journey. Help one another to stay awake and aware of the real life within.

Until you have found a group to share with, you can gain a great deal by reading other Enneagam material. Read at least one or two other sources. Each presenter is coming from a different perspective so there's always a new viewpoint to add to what you already have. It's helpful to see the differences even in presentations. This variety of presentations clearly demonstrates what the Enneagram theory describes as our nine different views of reality.

A DIFFERENT KIND OF GROWTH PROCESS

After you have spent much time "reunioning" with yourself, maybe even as long as a year, you'll probably still have the same question you had earlier. How do I change myself? The changing that takes place in the Enneagram process is different than any other change process we've been involved in before. In other growth work we've all become used to being told what we have to do. Then we grab onto our list or program. With the Enneagram growth process it's more a case of letting go. We have to:

— let go of the fear that something horrible is
   threatening our survival,

— let go of being afraid we may find something awful
   inside or even nothing inside,

— let go of the feeling that we're not worthy of our
   own attention,

— let go of holding the cover so tightly in place,

— let go of taking such great pride in our *idealized
   self-image,*

— let go of hiding our *avoidance,*

— let go of insisting that our way is the *only* way,

— let go of thinking that we can fix ourselves,

— let go of our limited impressions which suggest that
   thinking is the *only* way to know life, or that
   feeling is the *only* way to know "do life," or that
   reacting is the *only* way to be alive.

In place of what we formerly held onto so tightly, we will now need to embrace our avoidances:

The Ones will need to let go of their preconceived expectations and their resentments. They need to embrace life as a process filled with options and optimism and humor. To do this, they will have to risk being in process themselves.

The Twos will need to let go of giving before being asked and of giving beyond the request. They need to embrace their own neediness and risk sharing with others the great gift of their own woundedness.

The Threes will need to let go of producing and promoting their own products and themselves. They need to embrace their own greatest failure of not being real. In doing this, they will have to risk being found out as "less than advertised."

The Fours will need to let go of emotionally amplifying life in order to "create" special atmospheres. They need to embrace their own commonness and risk being seen by others in a way they feel is defective.

The Fives will need to let go of observing and thinking before living. They need to embrace their own emptiness, jump into life and get involved. Of course, they will have to risk being seen before they are ready for others to see just how little they know.

The Sixes will need to let go of always consulting others instead of taking responsibility for their own lives. They need to embrace their own inner authority, their own instincts and intuition. This will involve the risk of being caught out on a limb, so to speak, feeling unprepared for life.

The Sevens will need to let go of seeking continual sensations, tasting all with little digesting. They need to embrace their own inner pain and sadness. They must risk experiencing the deep and dark inside of reality.

The Eights will need to let go of relishing the struggle and the contrariness of wrestling with others and with life.

They need to embrace themselves and others, risking the display of tender and caring love.

The Nines will need to let go of their "peace at any price" contentment. They need to embrace their own conflictual feelings and begin making choices and stating preferences at the risk of offending others.

Do you get a sense of this new type and direction of growth? Enjoy whoever you find your original selves to be. Gradually let go of all that you once may have needed but now no longer need to survive. And finally, open to embrace what we have tried so hard to avoid. This new type of growth process is described well in the first chapters of *Enneagram Spirituality: From Compulsion to Contemplation*, by Suzanne Zuercher, O.S.B.

SOME RESULTS OF THIS NEW GROWTH PROCESS

We spoke earlier in Chapter Ten of the *arrowed lines of direction*. The most helpful way to use the information about the movement along the arrowed lines is to view this movement as the result of letting go. The movement along these arrowed lines should not be considered a plan for action. For example: The directions of the arrowed lines for the Number Fives are Seven and Eight. When we hear about "Five going to Eight," this *might* imply something the Fives try to do. *Instead,* it will be something that happens as a result of the Five letting go. A brief description may help. If the Fives can let go of hiding out and reading about life in order to get ready for life, then the Fives will naturally move into the swim of things. They will forthrightly move into life as the Eights do. This change in behavior for all of us may proceed little by little, but it will happen if we let go.

Another result of this new growth process has to do with the integration of the three centers: The Gut-Instinct Center, the Emotion-Motion Center, and the Cognitive Center. The ideal for all of us would be to live out of all three of these centers of our being at the same time. This would bring us to the integrated wholeness we are striving for. And yet when we locate ourselves on the Enneagram circle, we might see how strongly developed one center of our being is and how far removed we are from the other centers. If we are who we are from the beginning and we always remain the same Number, does this mean we will have to settle for being one-third of a person? Definitely not. It is only the strength and depth of our compulsion that holds us back from this wholeness. For example, if the Twos who feel that moving to meet peoples' needs is the only way they can effectively operate in life, they will never develop their cognitive side or their gut-instinct capacities to any great extent. However, as they begin to let go of their compulsive use of the natural gift of caring, they will begin to care for themselves. This will quite naturally lead to finding their own cognitive needs. Perhaps this will be done with the help of books, courses or study groups. The Two may also be more likely to get a body massage regularly or become active in a sport just for enjoyment. All these kinds of activities will awaken in the Two their other centers of being, and this will begin the integration process. It's important to remember that this integration did not start with the Twos taking up a new regimen for change. It began the day they first let go of their self-imposed compulsion to care for others at the expense of neglecting themselves.

TO BE FULLY ALIVE

Naturally, a few words will not suffice to describe an entire and wonderfully mysterious human being. Nor will all the Enneagram descriptions in the world be enough. There is still and always will be so much we don't know about our own humanness. However, we need to be aware of what we can know and understand so that we may more fully live and grow. As with all living creatures, unless we know who we are, we cannot create the climate necessary for growth. We cannot knowledgeably nourish our growth process. And if we don't know something of who we are, we will only become a small fraction of all that we were meant to be: fully human, fully gifted, fully alive.

A large part of what holds us back from our full personhood is simply not being aware of who we are. With the use of the Enneagram and the practice of self-observation, this self-awareness or self-remembering is quite possible. Another factor holding us back is our own resistance to meet ourselves honestly. As John Berryman, former poet laureate of Minnesota, once said, "We are as sick as we are secret." It follows from this that the positive approach would be: We are as healthy and whole as we are open and honest with ourselves. When we enter into a totally open and honest attitude toward ourselves, we cross a threshold into reality. All the pretense, not only for others but, more importantly, for ourselves, gradually falls away. We become for the first time fully free and whole. We stand naked before ourselves and God. It is vitally important in that moment to know that we are loved unconditionally. We are something like Quasimodo in the old classic movie *The Hunchback of Notre Dame* or Beast in the more recent movie *Beauty and the Beast.* Each of these characters tries to cover his disfigurement to gain acceptance or at least avoid rejection. As was true in these stories, it is only when we feel confident that we are lovable that we will risk uncovering ourselves.

We must begin with the belief that the God who created us and who has so richly gifted us truly loves us, cover and all. From the warmth of God's love we need to develop a truly compassionate love for ourselves. As someone once said, "We are the King's kids!" We have been royally gifted. However, we have also felt wounded. Because of this, we sought to protect ourselves from further woundedness. We created a covering to protect us and allow us to continue growing. We needed to do this. Such a defensive process is a necessary part of being human in this world. Another consequent but necessary part of the human growth process is to wake up somewhere along the journey of life and shake off the covers. If we refuse to engage ourselves in this stage of the process, then our journey will become a circular maze. We will continue to live but not grow. We will continue to walk, but we will be going in circles. We will keep doing what we've always done. And we will keep tripping on the same boulders that have always blocked our paths. We will be going nowhere. Nothing will change unless we cross the threshold into openness and honesty. We must begin the uncovering of our truly original God-gifted selves. Only this will bring us to the fullness of life.

A PERSONAL NOTE

Some years ago when I first began presenting the Enneagram, I did not like ending the course just as the participants were starting to find their Numbers. I wanted to see what would follow next for them on their lifegrowth journeys. So I began "Lifegrowth Journey Groups" as a follow-up. Needless to say, it has been very rewarding for me and I'm sure for many of the group members as well. I not only got the opportunity to see what happened next for people, but I also became a part of the process. For a Five, which I am, that has truly been a gift of life. The more I have offered to others, the more I have gained in return. I am very grateful to all of those people who have been and still are a part of our Lifegrowth Journey Groups. Because of the wealth of growth that has occurred in these groups I have decided to share with you this next part of the journey. I am currently working on a book to be titled *Continuing Your Enneagram Journey through Self-Remembering*. This book will focus on what we have done in these groups to promote and support each others' growth processes. I do believe this will be a great help as you continue your own Enneagram journey.

And now let me offer each of you something to tuck in your pocket for the continuation of your journey, a prayer from Dag Hammarskjold:

For all that has been, thank you.

For all that will be, yes.

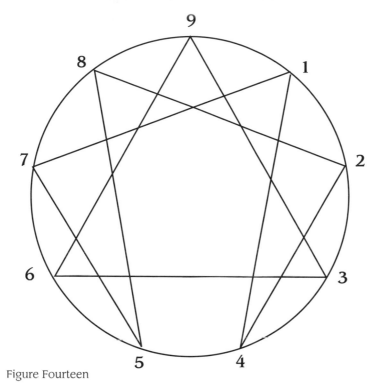

Figure Fourteen

Addendum

SELF-OBSERVATION QUESTIONS:

1. What is the compliment or affirmation you most like to receive?
2. What is the criticism you least want to receive?
3. When you're feeling good about yourself, what do you say to yourself?
4. When you're feeling down on yourself, what negative word or statement do you say to yourself?
5. What makes a day in your life a good day?
6. What makes a day in your life a bad day?
7. Would you say that your focus is mostly on people and relationships, or on ideas and factual information, or on the would as a whole?
8. With each new situation, what do you notice the most?
9. In each new situation, what do you instinctively do?
10. When faced with a possible threat or danger, what would be a typical reaction for you?
11. When you ask for directions, is it best for you to have someone tell you, or draw a map, or show you?
12. When you enter a room full of people you don't know, what do you think, feel, sense, or do?
13. How do you see yourself in relating to others?
14. How do you act when you are in charge of others?
15. How do you act when someone else is in charge of you or your activity?
16. How do you relate to, think of, or feel about work?
17. How do you relate to, think of, feel about time?
18. For you, what is the meaning and purpose of life?
19. How would you describe death in a symbolic way? Death is like . . .
20. How do you describe God?

Bibliography

This bibliography has been divided into two sections to help you choose appropriate sources for your particular stage on the journey. All those listed here have been developed by people who are various numbers on the Enneagram. Therefore, each will approach the topic from a different view of reality. You will probably find that some appeal to you more than others. The sources include books, cassette series, and a video series.

Some sources which describe the Enneagram theory and the Numbers:

Brady, Loretta. *The Enneagram: A Guide to Know Yourself and Understand Others* (video series). Allen, TX: Tabor Publishing, 1992.

Hurley, Kathleen V. and Theodore E. Dobson. *What's My Type?* San Francisco: Harper, 1991.

Kelley, Mary Helen, O.S.C. *Skin Deep (Designer Clothes by God).* Memphis, TN: Monastery of St. Clare, 1990.

O'Leary, S.J., Patrick. *Enneagram Basics* (cassette series). Kansas City, MO: Credence Cassettes, 1992.

Palmer, Helen. *The Enneagram: Understanding Yourself and the Others in Your Life.* San Francisco: Harper and Row, 1988.

Riso, Don Richard. *Personality Types: Using the Enneagram for Self-Discovery.* Boston: Houghton Mifflin Company, 1987.

Wagner, Jerome P. *The Enneagram Spectrum of Personality Styles.* Evanston, IL: self-published, 1993.

Zuercher, O.S.B., Suzanne and Dick Wright. *The Enneagram Cards: Sorting Out Your Space.* Notre Dame, IN: Ave Maria Press, 1994.

Some sources which provide opportunities for continuing growth:

Brady, Loretta and John Powell, S.J. *The Searchbook* (to accompany *Will the Real Me Please Stand Up?*). Allen, TX: Tabor Publishing, 1987.

Dobson, Ted and Kathy Hurley. *Breaking Through and Breaking Free* (cassette series). Kansas City, MO: Credence Cassettes, 1990.

Evans, Gloria Jay. *The Wall: A Parable.* Waco, TX: Word Books, 1977.

Henry, Kathleen. *The Book of Enneagram Prayers.* Jamaica Plain, NY: Alabaster Jar Liturgical Arts, 1987.

Kelley, O.C.S., Mary Helen. *Reality in Three Dimensions.* Memphis, TN: Monastery of St. Clare, 1992.

Metz, Barbara, S.N.D. de N. and John Burchill, O.P. *The Enneagram and Prayer.* Denville, NJ: Dimension Books, 1987.

Powell, John, S.J., and Loretta Brady. *Will the Real Me Please Stand Up?* Allen, TX: Tabor Publishing, 1985.

Riso, Don Richard. *Enneagram Transformations.* Boston: Houghton Mifflin, 1993.

Tart, Charles T. *Waking Up: Overcoming the Obstacles to Human Potential.* Boston: New Science Library, Shambhala, 1986.

Wagner, Jerome P. *Two Windows on the Self: The Enneagram and The Myers-Briggs* (cassette series). Kansas City, MO: Credence Cassettes, 1992.

Zuercher, Suzanne, O.S.B. *Enneagram Companions: Growing in Relationships and Spiritual Direction.* Notre Dame, IN: Ave Maria Press, 1993.

------ *Enneagram Spirituality: From Compulsion to Contemplation.* Notre Dame, IN: Ave Maria Press, 1991.

------ *The Enneagram, Personality and Prayer* (cassette series). Notre Dame, IN: Ave Maria Press, 1993.